NORDIC BABY CROCHET

CHARLOTTE KOFOED WESTH

NORDIC BABY CROCHET

Assembly-free patterns
for little ones

BATSFORD

Contents

: For novices
: For novices and crocheters with some experience
: For the experienced crocheter
: For the confident
: For the very confident

Preface

Welcome to my world of crochet

The patterns in this book are the result of more than a year's worth of labour. But this was a labour of love, where I've tried to create useful and stylish patterns for babies and toddlers up two years old. As you explore these patterns, you'll find that this is crochet in a new and somewhat different manner. I've found that, while there are many good books on knitted baby clothes, there has always been a gap when it comes to useful and well-thought-out crocheting patterns for the kinds of clothes and accessories you need in that first period after a baby is born.

Unfortunately, many people believe that crochet is impractical for clothing and choose knitting instead. Crochet has a reputation for being inelastic and dense – something that offers an advantage for amigurumi or when making items such as bags, oven mitts or blankets. However, crochet is good for other items too, and I hope that more people will discover the opportunities that crochet affords when it comes to making clothes for little ones.

I've tried to ensure that, with the patterns in this book and the right type of yarn, you will be able to discover all that crochet has to offer. I hope to guide you to achieving a nice finish as well as excellence in the finer details. I recommend that you read the opening chapters of the book before you start any project as it will be easier to follow the instructions if you first understand the construction and logic of the patterns. In those first chapters I share my observations on crochet as well as giving instructions on how to achieve a fluent crocheting flow so you can crochet better and for longer. I also include relevant tips such as how to hold the hook comfortably and how to achieve the correct stitch density for the patterns.

I've tried to design the baby clothes in the book with an ethos of simplicity that follows a consistent Nordic expression and style; one that is neither too flamboyant nor too cute. At the same time, I've tried to ensure that the clothes have a comfortable, elastic fit so that they are practical and suitable for day-to-day wear. Crocheting into the back loop creates a more elastic ribbed pattern that features in every pattern in the book. This also means that the clothes can be readily combined with each other.

Most of the clothes are crocheted in one piece, and are usually crocheted from the top down, but a few are crocheted from the bottom up.

I feel that I've really managed to pack this book with clothes and accessories for babies. As with many a labour of love, I found that once I started I just couldn't stop, and I particularly enjoyed 'nerding out' over different details and new designs.

It is such a pleasure to share these patterns
with the world. I hope you will use this book
extensively and that you'll pull it down from
the shelf again and again to make gifts for
baby showers and the like. I hope it will
inspire you to create fantastic items for
the little ones in your life, that it will help
you develop your own ideas and patterns,
and that it will produce many a meditative
crocheting session. Do share your crocheted
baby clothes on Instagram using the hashtags
#nordicbabycrocheting and
@charlottekofoedwesth.

With love,
Charlotte

Crochet facts

Crochet is done with a needle that has a hook on one end. It likely developed as an evolution of tambour embroidery, a kind of crochet embroidery where stitches are formed on the surface of a frame-mounted piece of fabric by pulling loops of thread repeatedly up through the fabric with a thin hook. I crochet slip stitches as a finishing touch on all the patterns in this book, and in this I was inspired by the original form of tambour embroidery.

Historians are unsure where in the world *crochet* originated. However, it is believed that tambour embroidery came to Europe from Asia during the 1700s. In the 19th century, crochet was widely adopted and became especially popular in England. Queen Victoria even taught herself to crochet after falling in love with a piece of Irish crochet work. Crocheters then mainly created artistic lace patterns that matched the beautiful lace knitwear of the time.

Crochet is often measured against knitting's many fine qualities and beautiful patterns – a historical comparison that I also tend to make. As such, crochet has often found itself in knitting's shadow when it comes to making clothing. However, I am both a knitter and a crocheter, and while knitting is always a safe choice when it comes to making baby clothes, I would love this book to demonstrate that crochet and knitting both have something valuable to offer and can often be used for similar purposes.

Throughout the 20th century, craftspeople would commonly crochet a bit of clothing here and there, and perhaps a few blankets, as well as practical items for the home. Especially after the world wars, it was more common to crochet practical rather than decorative items. A throw blanket was a classic item found in many homes, and in the 1950s and 60s it was popular to own a beautifully crocheted christening gown or a crocheted bridal dress. Crochet was especially popular in the 1970s, when crocheted bucket hats in colourful patterns were fashionable. I've tried to continue such traditions by designing a christening gown and two baby blankets for this book.

CROCHETING TECHNIQUES

Crochet is a technique in which a hook is used to pull yarn through stitches and loops, again and again. After a while, a coherent piece of crocheted fabric takes form that, with a bit of magic, can be shaped in different ways depending on how many and what kinds of stitches the fabric is composed of.

Crochet has four basic stitches: chain stitch, double crochet, slip stitch and treble crochet. Chain stitch is used to create the starting chain. Slip stitches are used to join one crocheted element to another and for tambour embroidery. Finally, double and treble crochet are crochet's answer to knitting's knit and purl stitches in that they can be used to create other variants of stitches.

All four stitches can be endlessly combined and varied. For example, I often use half treble crochet stitches – a variation of the treble crochet stitch – for the patterns in this book, and I've played with all four stitch variants throughout.

Something I also urge you to do when making these patterns is to experiment when you reach places in the design where one crochets straight up and down in rib. For example, you could swap half treble stitches with double crochet stitches, or swap treble crochet with half treble crochet or slip stitches and so on. In this way, you can easily vary the expression and overall appearance of the designs in the book to create unique pieces.

Try to make your stitches light and relatively loose, so the finished pieces are airy and soft. Picture the insulation in a house: if there is no air in the material, it won't keep the house warm and insulated as efficiently. It is the same for yarn. The biggest issue in crocheting is often that the stitches turn out too tight.

BEFORE YOU START

There are about 30 patterns in this book, and more than 40 different designs. There is a good mix of large and small projects of differing degrees of difficulty, and a wide range of baby clothing and other accessories.

Filippa's dress, along with a pair of baby shoes, became the first set that I crocheted for my sister's first grandchild. This inspired me to give all the other designs names too.

As a result, there are many names flying around in this book. However, I believe this makes referencing easier; when Thit's sweater or Sandra's blanket are mentioned it's clear exactly which design we mean. However, this doesn't exclude one from crocheting Thit's sweater for a boy or William's vest for a girl; most of the designs are intended to be unisex. Dresses and ruffles might be less common for boys but I say let it rip.

About the patterns

As a rule, I've crocheted all the designs in one piece. Most are crocheted from the top down, although in some cases you'll need to crochet from the bottom up or from side to side. Common to all, however, is that they don't need to be seamed. There are no ugly, thick seams and there is nothing that needs to be joined together when you crochet in one piece. At the most, you might need to reinforce a stitch when you fasten off or sew on a button. If there are pieces that need to be joined together it is done using slip stitches.

Projects that require joining often end up being abandoned because the process can be tedious and often gives rise to problems, especially if the parts don't fit seamlessly with one another. I'm sure many crocheters will be relieved that much of this challenging work is not required for the patterns in this book.

As mentioned, when crocheting top down, everything comes out in one piece and the construction of the design is considered from the start. This method ensures that your sweater, trousers or dress is complete once you've crocheted your last stitch. I even suggest that you weave in your yarn ends and sew on buttons as you go, letting you enjoy the work while also giving you the satisfaction of being able to dress the little one immediately once you are done.

In many of the patterns, I describe measuring off 1–5 metres of yarn before you crochet the first chain stitches. This is quite uncommon, but since the purpose of it is to avoid joining your work, I want to make sure you have a minimum of yarn ends to weave in. When you measure off yarn to use for edging and ties and so on from the start, you end up with only one end to fasten off instead of three or more.

If you are unfamiliar with crocheting from the top down it may feel somewhat new and different at first. However, you will quickly get used to it. It will also help if you try to visualise the shape and cut of the item you are crocheting and where you are in the design as you go. I also encourage you to sketch your own designs and ideas on paper before you start, so that you have a clear idea of your intended garment. As an example, look at Vidar's baby blanket (p. 208), where I've included an image that shows the colour scheme and where the crocheted blocks are placed.

It's always useful to get an overview of the method and the different steps of the pattern before you start. However, it is not my intention that you study the pattern in detail before beginning. That can often lead to more confusion than clarity.

When I mention the right and left on a design, I mean left and right as if the baby is wearing the design; therefore, the baby's left and right side.

The foundations and most of the intellectual work are done at the beginning of the project when you crochet starting from the top (for example from the neckline, shoulder or waist) and down to the bottom edge of the blouse, skirt, vest etc. Unfortunately, this method is a little slower than if you are used to crocheting from the bottom up because of the increases, the distribution of stitches plus the placement of different markers and so on, which may take you a while to get used to. Make sure you count the stitches at the beginning, ideally on every row where there are increases. Achieving the right shape and fit of the garment depends on having the correct number of stitches and achieving an even tension.

This method requires more counting at the start, but is still preferable to starting over. Soon you will be rewarded with plenty of 'TV crochet', where you can just get on with the project without having to give much thought to each row and round. 'TV crochet' is my term for when you can talk, watch TV or listen to audiobooks as you crochet.

I have only used increases in raglan and circular yokes when creating patterns that are made from the neckline down. Choose patterns with increases in round yokes if you have never tried the top-down method; this is easier than making raglan increases. You'll find eight patterns with raglan increases and 11 using increases in a round yoke in this book.

When you are crocheting raglan increases, use a contrasting colour of yarn for your markers that can be carried up with each row or round. Using yarn makes it much easier to see the progression in the diagonal increase line.

In these patterns, I have avoided using saddle shoulder construction, using the contiguous method for attaching sleeves, using balloon sleeves or anything like that. Those are all exciting techniques but better suited for different designs, even though I can see how those methods from knitting can all be applied to crochet. Knitting is extremely well suited for baby clothes, and with many of the patterns in this book I was inspired by knitted garments that have a beautiful shape or fit.

Working top down also means that the length of the body or the sleeves is easily adjusted while you work, and it's relatively easy to try the clothes on the baby as you go. Even easier, in fact, since there is only one stitch to keep hold of while you are fitting the garment.

The approach also lends itself well to projects where you think you may only have just enough yarn to finish. You can adjust the length during the project with the yarn that you have at your disposal. For many of the patterns I've also made it easy to lengthen the sleeves, legs and body later as the child grows.

I have used ribbing in all of the patterns. That requires crocheting in the back loop only, usually abbreviated as BLO. This gives a beautiful and elastic structure to the finished garments. To achieve the ribbed effect you must crochet BLO, alternating between the right side and the wrong side. With shoes, baskets, skirts and trousers where you crochet in rounds you therefore need to change direction on each round. In this manner, the stitches are alternated from the right/outer side to the wrong/inner side. I also use slip stitch rib, double crochet rib, half treble crochet rib and treble crochet rib.

I am very fond of single-colour designs. However, it is nice to step out a little, which is why I include a couple of patterns in spike stitch that both look nice and are easy to make. The spike stitch creates a bit more variation in colour and expression. It is an inherent advantage of spike stitch that it seems like you are crocheting with several colours while only working with one at any given time.

There is quite an intentional and uniform finish on all the designs as all the details have been thought through. I consistently use slip stitch for edging, but other techniques and stitches can also be chosen.

As mentioned before, the different designs can be combined freely as they share commonalities in technique and therefore match in terms of overall style and look. As I worked on the different designs I was often tempted to mix and match patterns, sleeve lengths, ruffles and edges. Therefore you have quite a few options. For example, you could

choose two colours rather than one when crocheting the rib patterns, or a blouse could be crafted with short sleeves rather than long ones. You could make a different style of ruffle or exclude the ruffle entirely. You could use a lighter, more summery, yarn even if the designs are listed using a heavy woollen yarn. You'll find other options and variants in the 'Tip' sections for the different designs. I encourage you to think of the patterns in this book as a starting point from which you can continue to develop your own ideas and designs. As an example, Amanda's dress (page 156) is a pattern that I've re-used for three very different dresses.

SIZES

Some patterns are for a single size while others have instructions for four to five sizes. In most of them, the sizes range from three months up to two years old. Bibs, moccasins and other accessories are usually in two or three sizes, whereas blankets and other items for a baby's room are one size. For caps it's important that they fit snugly, so there are six different sizes to choose between for something like Georg's cap. Of course it's best to get the child's exact measurements. Then again, children are unique and grow surprisingly fast – you might need to crochet a nine-month size for a six-month-old baby, for example.

DIFFICULTY

For each pattern I've included a key that describes how challenging it is: from one to five crochet hooks. Of course, this is also unique to the individual; what may be easy to some may be more challenging for others.

🪝: For novices
🪝🪝: For novices and crocheters with some experience

●●●: For the experienced crocheter
●●●●: For the confident
●●●●●: For the very confident

TENSION

It's important to start with a sample to ensure you have the tension correct before you embark on the whole pattern. If you achieve the correct tension, the pattern will work out to size and the end result won't be too dense. I recommend crocheting a trial square around 10cm × 10cm with the specific yarn and crochet hook size listed in the pattern instructions. Place the square on a flat surface and use a ruler to check your measurements.

STITCH HEIGHT

When you are crocheting in the back loop, the stitches will contract vertically quite a bit. How much depends on the type and elasticity of the yarn. Therefore, make sure to stretch your trial square a little before measuring. It's often useful to go up a half size, from 3mm to 3.5mm or from 3.5mm to 4mm, for example, so that you get a larger loop. If you find in your sample that there are more rows in your 10cm, then your stitches are too tight. If the stitch width is correct, try a longer loop with the hook as described in the section below about Crochet Flow. You can also try a larger hook.

If there are fewer rows, your stitches are too loose and you should try a smaller hook. You can also experiment with more tension and making the loop smaller on the hook.

STITCH WIDTH

If there are too many stitches in your 10cm, your stitches are too tight and small and you should perhaps try going up a hook size. Likewise, you can try to loosen your stitches a bit by making the loop larger on the hook.

If there are too few stitches, the tension is too loose, the stitches are too large and a smaller hook is called for. You can also increase tension by making the loops smaller on the hook.

CROCHET FLOW

It's important to try and cultivate a relaxed flow when crocheting. Crocheting is meant to be pleasurable. Find a cosy nook somewhere in your home. Seat yourself comfortably with a lamp that affords you a clear and bright light directly on your work. Personally, I find a light source from above and behind on my right side optimal. Good lighting is necessary when you are crocheting in the back loop using a dark yarn.

It's annoying if the yarn splits or if you manage to only partially draw the yarn through the loop. In crocheting, if you spot a problem once you are on to the next row there is no recourse but to unravel all your work until you reach the error and crochet the stitch again.

If you feel you have the hang of it and are consistently achieving the correct tension, you can skip this section. Alternatively, you can read on in the hopes that something in these pages will help evolve and develop your technique. Often I find that it only takes a single word or sentence to further your skill. I am still learning new things even after 40 years of crocheting.

Try not to exert yourself. Relax and lower your shoulders, holding the crochet hook lightly and gently. You will quickly tire if you grip too tightly as you work, and you don't want to end up with blisters on your fingers and a stiff neck and shoulders. You should be able to crochet for 12 hours with no issues. You'll ensure a good flow by leaving the loop relatively loose and long on the hook – looser than you'd imagine initially. Draw at your work with your left hand and pull down for every stitch so that the loop is loose on the hook. This is something of a balancing act, as you don't want everything too loose either.

However, the long, loose loops are important, as they affect the height of the stitch. I cannot emphasise this enough. In my experience, it's relatively easy to get the width of the stitches to match the tension of the pattern. However, it's often more difficult to get the stitch height right. If you end up on the short side, you'll have to crochet more rounds or rows to achieve the correct measurements. This will also make your piece more dense and compact and you'll have used up more yarn than necessary. Obviously it makes a huge difference to your garment if you can make do with 20 rows for 10cm instead of 25. Indeed, it's this 'density issue' that makes it important to achieve ease and flow in your work. You cannot just choose a larger hook, as even though your stitch heights will increase so will the width of your stitches.

TURNING STITCHES

Notice that I don't count turning stitches in the stitch totals for the patterns. This is the neatest and easiest method and will give you a more exact stitch count.

The chain stitches that you crochet at every row or round serve the purpose of raising you up to the same height as subsequent stitches. It creates a neat start to every row when the turning chains look something like a row of pearls on each side. When you crochet in rounds, the turning stitches act as filler, so the crochet looks tight and neat in the joins.

See the images opposite for the exact stitches that you'll need to create straight joins in your work.

Typically you turn with one chain stitch before crocheting a double crochet, two chain stitches before a half treble crochet or three chain stitches before a treble crochet stitch.

HOW AND WHEN YOU CROCHET THE VARIOUS STITCHES

As mentioned earlier, you will create a rib effect when crocheting into the back loop. Many of the patterns call for you to turn and crochet in the opposite direction after every round/row. In other words, you'll be crocheting from the right and the wrong side alternately as you go. This is done even if you are following the body of a blouse or a sleeve all the way around. It's important that you are aware of exactly which stitch to crochet in at the first and last stitch. Otherwise you risk the joint under the sleeve or down the length of the body wobbling or pulling crooked as you inadvertently increase or decrease the number of stitches each turn.

Crocheting in both loops. This is the standard way of crocheting.

Crocheting in the front loop only (FLO).

Crocheting in the back loop only (BLO) of the first stitch of a row.

Crocheting in the back loop only (BLO) of the final stitch of a row.

Crocheting in the back loop only (BLO) of the first stitch when working back and forth in rounds.

Crocheting in the back loop only (BLO) of the final stitch of a round.

Closing a round. Slip stitch (sl st) both loops of the first stitch.

Placement of stitch markers – yarn can be carried forward along the line of increases to show the progression.

Decreasing in this book involves completing two stitches as one.

Increasing involves working two stitches into one stitch of the previous row.

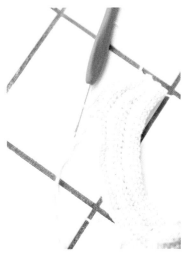

Fan increase – a double increase that is crocheted from the right side with three stitches worked through both loops of the stitch of the previous row. It looks like a fan or a tulip.

Spike stitch is worked like double crochet but into a stitch two or three rows below for a two-colour pattern.

Tools and materials

The patterns in this book are crocheted in a selection of quality yarns that are fine, light and soft. Baby clothes should feel comfortable and soft against a baby's delicate skin. Lean towards using natural materials, although you can choose to add a few synthetic fibres to help maintain the colour and shape of the garment. The yarn should be pleasant to crochet with and able to withstand laundering as well as ordinary wear and tear. For baby clothes it's also important not to use yarn that sheds long fibres that can get into a baby's eyes and mouth. Longer-haired varieties of yarn with a tendency to fluff and tangle, for example silk/mohair blends, should be avoided for the youngest ones. Eco and GOTS certified yarn is sustainable and good for both the child and the environment.

For maternity gifts, I highly recommend a cotton/wool blend. The mix of wool and cotton is suitable for both summer and winter, as long as the sizing is spot on and the clothes are neither too large nor too tight.

I would recommend shopping for yarn in a physical store, partly for the advice and expertise on hand, and partly because you get to see and feel the different types of yarn. Choose something you are drawn to, such as a beautiful colour or a particularly light and luxurious feel to the yarn, which will work for what you wish to crochet. Remember, it is often pleasure that motivates crochet, and while online stores are wonderful if you already know what you need, a physical shop offers more to the senses. Indeed, many of the garments in this book were inspired by yarn I've held in my hands.

YARN RECOMMENDATIONS

Gepard
Cotton Wool 3 Organic: 50% wool and 50% cotton. 230 metres/50g:
Alma's tunic, Anton's nappy pants, Freja's skirt, Filippa's dress, William's vest, Karl Viggo's trousers, Georg's cap & mittens, Dagmar's elephant rattle.

Linen Unika: 100% extra fine linen, 160 metres/50g:
Leo's christening gown, Lulu's christening bonnet, Holger's pacifier cord, Aske's bib.

My Fine Wool: 100% superfine merino. 233 metres/50g:
Alma's tunic, Anton's nappy pants, Karl Viggo's trousers, Georg's cap & mittens.

Isager
Merilin: 80% wool and 20% linen. 208 metres/50g:
Otto's cardigan.

Alpaca 1: 100% alpaca. 400 metres/50g:
Olga's sweater, Jens' & Julie's tops, Antony's tunic

Önling

No 2: 100% superfine merino. 120 metres/25g:
Manna's moccasins, Vidar's baby blanket.

No 11: 90% superfine merino and 10% cashmere. 180 metres/25g:
Milla's blouse, Anton's nappy pants.

No 12: 55% wool, 45% cotton. 800 metres/115g:
Filippa's dress, Freja's skirt, Karl Viggo's trousers.

No 14: 78% cotton and 22% linen. 125 metres/50g:
Erik's jacket

Onion

Organic cotton: 100% organic cotton. 155 metres/50g:
Ester's cardigan.

Sandnes

Alpaca Silk: 70% baby alpaca and 30% mulberry silk. 200 metres/50g:
Alexander's bodysuit.

Sunday: 100% merino. 235 metres/50g:
Anton's nappy pants, Anni's T-shirt, Amanda's dress.

Babyull Lanett: 100% merino wool, 175 metres/50g:
Jens' & Julie's tops.

Tynn Line: 53% cotton, 33% viscose and 14% linen. 220 metres/50g:

Anni's T-shirt, Amanda's dress, Peer Bo's sunhat.

Sandnes Tynn Merinoull: 100% merino wool. 175 meters/50g:
Sandra's baby blanket.

Rowan
Rowan Finest: 50% wool, 20% cashmere, 30% alpaca. 87 meters/25g:
Jens' & Julie's tops.

Cotton Glacé: 100% mercerized cotton. 115 meter/50g:
Philip's basket, Jack's cloth.

Krea Deluxe
Organic Cotton: 100% organic cotton. 165 meters/50g:
William's vest, Ashe's bib, Berthine & Helene's collars, Dagmar's elephant rattle, Holger's pacifier cord, Jack's cloth, Dagmar's elephant rattle.

Organic Wool 1: 100% organic wool. 145 meters/50g:
Jens & Julie's tops.

Fru Krogh
Cashmere blend hand dyed yarn: baby alpaca, cashmere, silk and merino. 400 meters/100g:
Emmy's Dress.

Permin
Elise Cotton Cashmere: 90% cotton and 10% cashmere. 115 meters/25g:
Eva's romper, Leo's christening gown, Lulu's christening bonnet.

Drops
Brushed Alpaca Silk: 23% silk, 77% alpaca. 140 meters/25g:
Lucia's top.

Cotton Light: 50% cotton and 50% polyester. 105 meters/50g:
Bjørn's cover for baby carrier

Askeladen
Lanolin yarn: 100% lanolin wool.
Nipple shield (included under 'tip' in the pattern for Jack's burp cloth).

Cewec
Tibet Yak Merino: 24% yak, 55% merino wool and 21% polyamide. 190 metres/25g:
Thit's sweater, Agnes Marie's Christmas dress.

Hot Socks Pearl:
75% merino wool, 20% polyamide and 5% cashmere. 200 metres/50g:
Amanda's dress (winter version).

Filcolana
Anina: 100% superwash merino. 210 metres/50g:
Freja's skirt, Karl Viggo's trousers, Filippa's dress, Alma's tunic.

Lang Yarns
Nova Merino Camel: 48% merino wool, 32% camel wool and 20% polyamide. 180 metres/25g:
Thit's sweater, Agnes Marie's Christmas dress.

You will find further information about colours as well as yarn quantities and tension in the specific patterns where the yarn is used. If you search for the different brands on the internet, you should be able to find nearby shops that stock what you need.

Make sure you check the colour specifications of the yarn and always use the same dye lot of yarn so your garment has a consistent colour from top to bottom.

If you are new to crochet, make sure you follow the yarn recommendations in the patterns to ensure a good result. If you are a more experienced crocheter it is easier to swap one type of yarn for another, but as yarn can behave quite differently it's important to know what you are doing here. For many of the patterns I have included other recommendations for yarn to work with, although some are more specific than others. You'll find these in the patterns themselves or under 'Tip'. Jens' and Julie's tops, for example, can be crocheted with many different types of yarn with consistently good results. Likewise, for Anton's nappy pants I have included three different yarn types to choose between. All the yarn types I've included here were available when the book was published.

Clover Amour has a smaller hook and can get through a knitting needle gauge. This is rarely possible with other brands, which often have a slightly thicker hook than its handle.

CROCHET HOOKS

In my experience, the best crochet hooks are from Clover. They have a smooth hook with a satin-like finish that ensures the yarn doesn't stick to the hook. Further, the hook is relatively small, which allows it to easily glide into each stitch. They will last you forever as long as you wield them softly and lightly while you crochet.

Choose either Clover Soft Touch, which is copper coloured (with a silicon dot for your thumb that makes it particularly well suited to an underhand grip) or Clover Amour, which is covered in a silicon sheath and comes in different colours depending on the size of the hook. Amour is one centimetre longer (14cm) than Soft Touch (13cm), which makes it better suited for an overhand grip or for larger hands.

It's important that the yarn you choose works for the hook you are using, with its size dependent on the quality, thickness and spin of the yarn. Usually you'll find recommendations for which size knitting

needles to use on the yarn's label, but not always the size of the recommended crochet hook. Often you can choose a hook slightly larger than the recommended knitting needle – usually a half to a whole size larger, as with crocheting you'll pull the yarn around itself more times, which will make everything a bit more dense.

If the yarn is quite tightly spun or has a lot of elasticity, a larger hook will also help loosen everything a little so the result isn't quite so dense. Read more about tension and density on page 15 as well as cultivating a relaxed crochet flow, also on page 15.

All the patterns in this book are crocheted with hooks ranging between 2.5mm and 4.5mm.

Note: when you are crocheting you should use the hook size specified for the pattern. The thick part of the metal handle is the diameter specified in millimetres. Knitting needles use the same system, with thicknesses specified at 3mm, 3.5mm or 4mm and so on. A 4mm

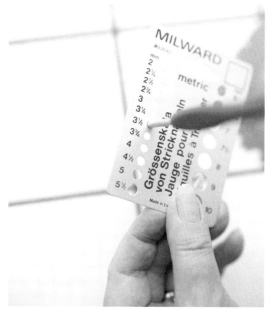

Prym crochet hook gauge.

A crochet hook measured on a knitting-needle gauge.

crochet hook, in other words, has the same thickness as a 4mm knitting needle.

Sizes are specified in millimetres, which equates to international standards. If you use American or older British hooks that use different number systems, check which size equates to the metric size specified.

For every stitch the loop should slide easily back and forth on the thickest part of the metal portion of the hook. You won't get the work to flow with ease if the loop only reaches the hook part of the crochet hook. The loop will end up too small and the work will be more difficult than it needs to be.

HOLDING THE HOOK

Should you use an overhand or an underhand grip? Recently I read that the correct way to hold the hook is using the underhand grip. This puzzled me somewhat, as there is no single correct way; the choice is up to you.

The underhand grip is probably considered the traditional or old-fashioned method of crocheting.

What is most important is to find a rhythm that feels easy and enjoyable, that allows you to control the tension of the yarn as well as control the loop on the hook and the garment without tensing your hands or shoulders.

I hold the hook in an overhand grip, even though my grandmother taught me the traditional way. In other words, I hold the needle in the same way I would a knitting needle, in a grip many refer to as a 'knife grip'.

Using this grip, I hold the hook inside my hand with three fingers (pinky, ring finger and middle finger). This frees my index finger and thumb to create a pincer grip with which I guide and help the loop into its correct position on the front part of the hook.

Overhand grip.

Underhand grip.

My left hand regulates the yarn, using my pinky to ensure the yarn is free as the garment or item advances. The thumb and middle finger ensure that the crochet work is pulled down and the loop is pulled slightly larger so you have easy access and can see what you are doing while making sure that what you've crocheted doesn't spin around on the hook. I find that this gives me full control over every stitch.

When you employ an underhand grip, you hold the hook with your index finger and thumb (some use their middle finger for support). This places your two or three surplus fingers underneath, which makes it hard for these fingers to help control anything at the furthest point of the hook. The hook rests on top of the hand, between your index finger and thumb, much like you'd hold a pencil or pen. As a result, this is often referred to as a 'pencil grip'.

Some English people hold the right knitting needle with an underhand grip, so it's possible that its origin lies in England where crocheting has been popular historically.

Eventually you'll settle into your own way of doing things. It's only as a teacher that I really became conscious of all the different methods and their respective advantages and disadvantages. I find that you have a lot more manoeuvrability, command and strength to control materials such as fabric yarn and paper yarn when you use an overhand grip, so if you are a novice with no preconceived preferences I recommend you start with that.

When you've just started a project it can be difficult to control as there are only a couple of chain stitches to grip and hold on to. Many will find that supporting the hand with a small cushion, cloth or the like is helpful in these early stages.

When it comes to counting stitches, rounds and rows I prefer to keep track by jotting down numbers and lines on paper. Others prefer to use devices such as digital counters.

Something to support your hand during the start of a project.

OTHER TOOLS

Wool needles, a pair of scissors, plastic or yarn stitch markers, a measuring tape and a short ruler around 15–20cm are all useful things to have on hand. The ruler is useful when measuring tension, rib and edges. It's easier to control a ruler than a measuring tape. However, a measuring tape is useful when crocheting larger items. Choose one that extends and retracts.

Make sure you have a notebook to keep track of notes on the patterns, sizes, choice of yarn, measurements, number of stitches, increases and decreases and so on.

Do you want ruffles? And if so, where do you want them? And what kind of edges do you want? Keeping track of this sort of detail is useful if you've put a project aside for a while and are picking it up again.

Tip

When you put your project aside for a while, you can place a plastic stitch marker in the loop so your project doesn't unravel.

Tip

Unravel the last stitch when picking up a project again. This last stitch has often been pulled in a bit so that it is shorter than the other stitches. Unfortunately this can be quite apparent in the finished piece, especially when you are creating ribbed patterns.

Finishing

Finishing is the term we use to describe the overall appearance and finesse of the garment. It's also the term I use for adding the last round of detailing and polish on a project.

WEAVING IN ENDS

It's easier to weave in ends in crochet than in knitting. When crocheting you can simply hide the yarn ends in the stitches, which isn't possible when knitting.

Use a needle with a round point, like a wool needle. A sharp point can damage and cut through the fibres of the yarn.

The end of the yarn needs to be brought through 4–6 stitches in two rounds. When you are bringing the yarn back on the second round the yarn should knot around itself.

The slicker the yarn, the easier it is for the yarn to separate so the ends unravel. Make sure you are extra thorough if you are working with materials such as silk, viscose or Tencel.

It's useful to weave in your ends and sew on buttons as you go – it helps with motivation when the garment looks good throughout the project. You also get the satisfaction of having a finished garment as soon as you've crocheted the last stitch.

EDGES

You can add extra personality to the garments by using different edges, ruffles, patterns and bobbles.

Tambour embroidery

As mentioned previously, tambour embroidery is a predecessor to crocheting, where yarn is pulled in and out of the piece from the right side. It consists of chain stitches that are methodically crocheted through many stitches or between stitches if you want to add decoration to edges or, for example, to raglan slits or the rattle's elephant ears (page 200).

Tambour embroidery creates a row of unbroken slip stitches on the right side. I use the technique for features like finishing edges at the bottom of dresses, blouses, trousers and the like, where the slip stitches create a fuller and more pronounced edge. The slip stitches can also be used to tighten a slit or an edge if needed.

Slip stitches are actually chain stitches where you pull the yarn up through a crocheted surface. The result resembles embroidered chain stitches. This means you can use the technique to crochet letters and numbers or other designs onto the garment itself if you feel so inclined. However, I've only used slip stitch in these patterns to give our edges a nicer finish.

Stitching words with tambour embroidery.

On all the garments with a neck opening that doesn't have a ribbed neckline I crochet slip stitches for edges. This makes for a fuller and softer neckline. It's important that the slip stitches aren't too tight unless explicitly stated in the instructions. Use a hook that's a half or whole size larger if you feel the stitches are on the tighter side.

Tip

I crochet slip stitches by pulling the yarn through the work in two stages: first through the piece or the loop itself, then through the loop on the hook. In this way you can avoid tightening the yarn and the stitch too much.

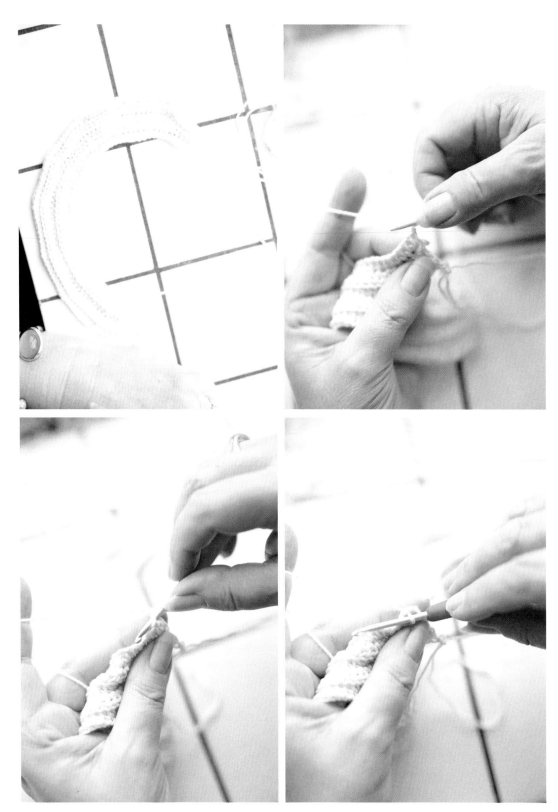

Using slip stitch to work yarn ends into the neckline.

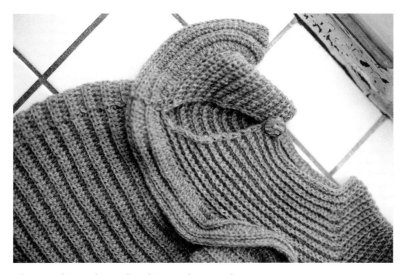

Slip stitching along the slit in Filippa's dress.

Crab stitch

Crab stitches are double crochet stitches crocheted in reverse. In other words, you crochet them from left to right. Crab stitches result in a thick, twisty edge.

Picot

Picot stitches are also known as 'mouse edges' in Danish.

Crochet *1 dc in the piece, 3 ch, 1 dc in 3rd chain stitch from the hook, skip 1 or 2 stitches on the piece*, rep from * to *.

The stitches will be tighter if you skip one stitch instead of two.

Crab stitches.

Picot.

Different types of ruffles.

Ruffles and bobbles

If you want to transfer bobbles or ruffles to a different garment than the ones I've included in this book you can find instructions in the patterns I've listed below.

Bobbles are described in Jack's cloth, p. 222, Philip's baskets, p. 218 and Ashe's bib, p. 174.

Ruffles on the rear are described in the instructions for Anton's nappy pants, p. 80. You can also make a tiny ruffle on the rear. Ruffles on the yoke are described in several patterns. I've crocheted ruffles on jerseys, vests, tunics and dresses, but a sweater or blouse could have ruffles on the yoke. Be aware that a jersey is open and the ruffles have to be crocheted back and forth. On Lucia's top, p. 116, and Ester's cardigan, p. 66, the ruffle is crocheted back and forth. On Filippa's dress, p. 48, and Alma's tunic, p. 38, the ruffle is joined and you crochet around.

A peplum on the bottom edge is described in the pattern for Milla's blouse, p. 42, and Julie's top, p. 102. This ruffle can also be used for finishing on sleeves, short or long. If you want short sleeves to have a ruffle, you can skip crocheting the decreases described for the sleeves.

A tiny ruffle for the neckline is described in Alexander's bodysuit, p. 140.

BUTTONS

There are buttons on many of the garments included in this book. There is no specific rule as to which side the buttonholes are placed. My attitude is that it doesn't really matter if the buttons are placed on the left or the right side, regardless of whether the garment is intended for a boy or a girl. I am a proponent of more unisex designs.

I often use mother-of-pearl buttons (roughly 1.5cm in diameter). Whether you use the more rustic-looking back of the button or the smooth front is up to you. The buttons are simple and pretty and don't take up too much space on the clothes themselves. If possible, sew the buttons on with the same yarn that you used to crochet the garment. Split the yarn into two or three threads if possible.

Many of the patterns have only a single button. I suggest you recycle something from a box of old buttons if you have one. It is a wonderful feeling to find the perfect button in the perfect colour.

GARMENT ELASTIC

There are 12 patterns in which I use garment elastic. I consistently use elastic instead of crocheted ties. It makes the clothes fit better and it makes them more comfortable to wear. Garment elastic comes in many different colours and widths, so choose the colour you prefer. Personally I prefer the coloured versions to the classic white elastic. I generally use a width of around 1.5cm. However, If you find the perfect colour, other widths will usually work too. I suggest you experiment here. You can also use coloured elastic used for swimwear and underwear, or you could swap in anorak elastic and stoppers where it makes sense and doesn't cause discomfort for the baby when lying down. Pull the elastic in and out between stitches as described in the patterns. At the end, double the elastic and finish it by tying a knot.

STEAMING, PRESSING AND LAUNDERING YOUR CROCHETED GARMENTS

Laundering deserves a chapter in its own right. It's not always necessary to wash your new baby clothes before giving them to their intended recipient. Typically you want the clothes to look and feel new and unused when gifting them. However, you will want to press the clothes to achieve that new look, which you can do by steaming under a dry cloth.

Iron and steam your clothes under a clean tea towel or a similar piece of fabric. Never iron

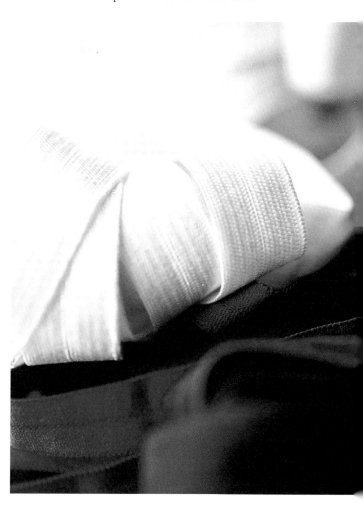

directly on the clothing itself. Likewise, don't apply too much pressure, as it will destroy the crocheted texture and surface of the garment. Always iron lightly over any ribbed edges. Be careful and experiment with the particular garment and quality of yarn.

It's not necessary to invest in special equipment to mount and stretch out the clothes.

I always recommend washing the clothes before you use them.

If you are gifting a garment, make sure you give the recipient clear instructions on how to wash it. You can include the yarn label with washing instructions in the gift too.

The first wash will cause the yarn to soften and fold itself out. This will also wash out any dirt, leftover spinning oil and surplus dye.

Use a conditioning wool detergent for any hand-worked garment made out of yarn, regardless of whether it's wool or cotton. Look for detergents with lanolin, a natural fat found in wool.

If you've crocheted a garment using several different colours, I recommend soaking your item in a little water and vinegar for about an hour before washing it. This will prevent the colours from bleeding into each other. You can leave cotton or linen to soak for a little longer.

I always wash crocheted items in the washing machine on a cold gentle cycle, preferably in a wash bag. Wash the item on its own, without other clothes, or the item may tangle up due to friction with other clothes. I insist on machine washing everything, with no exceptions, even if the yarn label specifies it can only be hand-washed. Wool, viscose,

Tip

You can buy special colour catcher cloths that are designed to pick up excess colour in the washing machine.

Water and vinegar softens cotton cloths, collars and bibs and helps them absorb more easily.

Tencel and silk do not tolerate sudden changes in temperature very well. This can become an issue, for example, if you are washing something at 30°C, and the rinsing takes place in ice-cold water. This can cause the garment to shrink and tangle.

Wool can handle very hot water of up to 90°C, but cannot tolerate temperature changes or heavy-handed treatment. Most washing machines rinse using cold water, which means washing something at 30°C and then rinsing it in cold water won't work, especially in winter when the water is icy cold. Only superwash-treated yarn can withstand this treatment. Therefore, always wash wool using cold water and at the lowest spin speed. You can wash items using a wool program, but make sure you set it to cold wash. If you have a washing machine that rinses at the same water temperature as it washes, there is usually no problem. If you are unsure what your washing machine does, you can experiment by washing a sample first. It's a shame to ruin a finished piece just because of the settings on a washing machine.

When drying your crochet, do not hang it up, as it will stretch and grow in size. Dry the wet baby clothes on a clean towel on the drying rack. Straighten the shape to the

desired measurements and leave it until dry.
Do not dry your clothes on the radiator either.
If your dryer has a warm air wool finish or
smoothing program, you can tumble the
crocheted baby clothes for five minutes just
before they are completely dry. This will
give a fuller, smoother and more luxurious
finish to the clothes. If necessary, check the
dryer after two minutes to make sure that
everything is fine and that the clothes are not
getting tangled.

ABBREVIATIONS

BLO	back loop only
ch	chain
ch st	chain stitch
dc	double crochet
dec	decrease
FLO	front loop only
htr	half treble crochet
inc	increase
PM	place marker
rem	remaining
rep	repeat
RS	right side
sl st(st)	slip stitch(es)
st(s)	stitch(es)
tog	together
tr	treble crochet
WS	wrong side

BABY CLOTHES

Alma's tunic

This beautiful tunic is indispensable for a baby. Alma's tunic is worked from the top down in one piece with raglan increases, half treble crochet and a flounce on the yoke and treble crochet on the bottom. There is a slit following the raglan line on the left side of the tunic at the back. The Gepard yarn is available in a variety of beautiful colours.

Size
3 (6) 9 (12) 24 months

Measurements
Length: 26 (31) 36 (38) 40cm
Width: 47 (55) 61 (67) 71cm

Yarn
Gepard My Fine Wool, 100% superfine merino, 233 metres/50g
Colour: 530 light grey
Quantity: 100 (150) 150 (200) 200g
For alternative yarns, see Tip on page 40.

Other materials
1 mother-of-pearl button approx. 1.5cm in diameter

Crochet hook
3mm

Tension
28 htr BLO x 19 rows = 10 x 10cm

Note
Make sure that you work the very last st on a row; it can be hard to find when working in BLO.
Turning chains do not count towards the total stitch count.
Mark raglan increases with stitch markers as explained in pattern.
Let the stitch markers (preferably yarn in a contrasting colour) be carried forward for each row.
The first inc of the two worked around the stitch marker is worked in st just above the stitch marker.

Pattern
Work all sts in BLO from row 2 unless otherwise stated in pattern.

Tip

For a more discreet ruffle, work a single round: Work round 1 and sl st edge.

YOKE

Leave approx. 2 metres of yarn hanging at beg, which you will use to finish neckline and add button loop. Work sl st as soon as you can. You then avoid having the yarn hanging during the rest of the work. Work 1 sl st in every st from RS with long end from cast-on, work 5 ch for button loop. Fasten the 5ch with 1 sl st a little further down the slit. Work sl sts further around the edge of the slit.

Work 62 (68) 76 (86) 88 ch.

Row 1 (RS): 1 htr in 3rd ch from hook, 1 htr in every subsequent ch (60 (66) 74 (84) 86 htr). Turn.

Work in BLO from now on.

Row 2 (WS): 2 ch, 2 htr in 1st htr (inc), 8 (9) 11 (12) 13 htr (shoulder), inc 1, PM, inc 1, 18 (20) 22 (26) 26 htr (front piece), inc 1, PM, inc 1, 8 (9) 11 (12) 13 htr (shoulder), inc 1, PM, inc 1, 18 (20) 22 (26) 26 htr (back), inc 1, (68 (74) 82 (92) 94 sts). Turn.

Rep row 2 with inc on every row a total of 10 (12) 14 (14) 16 times. Inc 8 sts on every row. As the stitch count increases on every row, the number of stitches between the increases will also go up. After inc there are 140 (162) 186 (196) 214 sts in total.

Finish yoke with a single row of htr without inc. Join at the end of this row to form a ring with 1 sl st in 1st htr through both loops.

BODY

Turn and work the opposite way for each of the body rounds. Even though you will be working tr in the future, turn with 2 ch. Continue to work over sts on back and front piece (body), skipping shoulder sts within ch. Remember to continue working in BLO.

Round 1 (WS): ch 2, 40 (46) 52 (56) 60 tr (back), 6 (8) 8 (10) 10 ch (armhole), skip shoulder sts, 40 (46) 52 (56) 60 tr (front piece), 6 (8) 8 (10) 10 ch (armholes), skip shoulder sts, close round with 1 sl st in 1st tr through both loops, (92 (108) 120 (132) 140 sts). Turn.

Round 2 (RS): ch 2, inc 1 (with dc) in 1st st, 1 tr in next st, *inc 1, 1 tr *, rep from * to * to 6 (8) 8 (10) 10 ch armholes in which 1 tr is worked, rep from * to * to 6 (8) 8 (10) 10 ch armholes in which 1 tr is worked. Close round with 1 sl st in 1st tr through both loops (132 (154) 172 (188) 200 sts). Turn.

Round 3: Ch 2, 1 tr in each st, close round with 1 sl st in 1st tr through both loops (132 (154) 172 (188) 200 sts). Turn.

Rep round 3 until piece measures 23 (28) 33 (35) 37cm or desired length. Then work 6 rounds of htr. Finish the edge from RS: 1 sl st in every st through both loops. Break yarn and finish off.

FLOUNCE

Now work a flounce in htr rib on yoke over 4 rounds. Work from RS in the free front

Tip

Gepard Cotton Wool 3 and Filcolana Anina also work well for this pattern.

stitches (you may work through both stitches on shoulder stitches). Make sure the neckline is pointing down so you are working in the right direction.

Round 1 (RS): slip yarn to back of any st on round flush with shoulder st, ch 2, htr 1 in same st, htr 2 in each st all around, close round with 1 sl st in 1st htr through both loops (280 (324) 372 (392) 428 sl sts). Turn and work the other way round.

Round 2: ch 2, 1 htr (remember BLO) in every st, close round with 1 sl st in 1st htr through both loops. Turn.

Rep round 2 1 (1) 1 (2) 2 times; then there are 3 (3) 3 (4) 4 rounds in total.

Finally work a sl st edge on flounce from RS.

FINISHING

Weave in any remaining ends and sew on button. Gently steam and press tunic under a dry cloth.

Tip

For a stitch variation, the body of Alma's tunic can be worked in half treble crochet or double crochet.

Milla's blouse

This blouse with short sleeves and a peplum is worked in one piece, in double crochet and half treble, with a slit in the centre back and a raglan neckline. The blouse is worked in superfine merino and cashmere from Önling. It is a light, lovely soft yarn with a long run length.

Sizes
3 (6) 9 (12) 24 months

Measurements
Chest width: approx. 46 (50) 54 (58) 60cm
Full length: approx. 24 (26) 29 (31) 34cm

Yarn
Önling No 11, 90% superfine merino and
10% cashmere, 180 metres/25g
Quantity: 50 (50) 75 (75) 100g

Other materials
1 mother-of-pearl button: approx. 1.5cm in
diameter

Crochet hook
3.5mm

Tension
26 htr BLO x 16 rows = 10 x 10cm

Note
Make sure you are working the very last
st on a row; it can be hard to find when
working BLO.
Turning chains are not counted in the total
stitch count.
Mark raglan increases with stitch markers as
explained in the pattern.
Let the stitch markers (preferably yarn in a
contrasting colour) be carried forward for
each row.
The first of the two increases worked around
the stitch marker is worked in sts just above
the stitch marker.

Pattern
Work all sts BLO from row 2 unless
otherwise stated in pattern.

*The blouse worked in Önling
No 11 is shown on page 45. This
alternative version was worked in a
hand-dyed yarn from Sysleriget.*

Tip

Use yarn alternatives, such as sock yarn or hand-dyed yarn. Just make sure you stick to the tension indicated in the pattern. Yarns with a running length of 210 metres/50g are suitable for this model. Quantity needed is: 100 (100) 150 (150) 200g.

YOKE

Leave approx. 2 metres of yarn hanging at the beginning; you will need this to work the neckline. Work sl st as soon as you can to avoid having the yarn hanging during the rest of the work. This is done as follows:
With the long end from the cast-on, work 1 sl st in every st from RS, work 5 ch for button loop, and fasten with 1 sl st a little further down the slit.

Work 71 (77) 83 (87) 87 ch.
Row 1 (RS): 1 dc in 2nd ch from hook, 1 dc every subsequent ch (70 (76) 82 86 (86) sts). Turn.

If you like, put a stitch marker on RS so you know where you are in the piece.

Row 2 (WS): ch 1, work dc BLO, and at the same time divide piece with stitch markers into front, back and sleeves as follows: 13 (15) 16 (16) 16 sts (back piece), PM, 10 (10) 11 (12) 12 sts (sleeve), PM, 24 (26) 28 (30) 30 sts (front piece), PM, 10 (10) 11 (12) 12 sts (sleeve), PM, 13 (15) 16 (16) 16 sts (back piece), (70 (76) 82 86 (86) sts). Turn.

Row 3: ch 1, work dc, and inc in st before and after each marker. Work a total of 8 incs on this row = 8 extra sts (78 (84) 90 (94) 94 sts). Turn.

Row 4: ch 1, dc 1 in every st in row (78 (84) 90 (94) 94 sts). Turn.

Row 5: Ch 1, dc to end, and at the same time inc 1 on each side of each marker (86 (92) 98 (102) 102 sts). Turn.

Row 6: ch 1, dc 1 in each st (86 (92) 98 (102) 102 sts). Turn.

Row 7: Ch 1, dc and inc 1 on each side of each marker (94 (100) 106 (110) 110 sts). Turn.

Row 8: ch 1, dc 1 in each st of row (94 (100) 106 (110) 110 sts). Turn.

Row 9: ch 1, dc 1 (continue BLO) in first 6 sts, then htr (BLO), and inc on each side of each marker, finish with dc 1 in last 6 sts (102 (108) 114 (118) 118 sts). Turn.

Rep row 9 another 9 (10) 11 (12) 13 times until you have a total of 18 (19) 20 (21) 22 rows on yoke. There are 174 (188) 202 (214) 222 sts divided into 26 (29) 31 (32) 33 sts for back, 36 (38) 41 (44) 46 sts for sleeve, 50 (54) 58 (62) 64 sts for front, 36 (38) 41 (44) 46 sts for sleeve and 26 (29) 31 (32) 33 sts for back.

For sizes 6 months and 12 months, work an extra row without inc. This is to ensure that the double crochet rib fits when continuing on sleeves and body. Break yarn and finish off.

BODY

Divide sts on 1st round so that body can now be worked in the round in one piece and sleeves can be finished separately later.

Round 1 (RS): slip the yarn in the first st of one half of the back (just after the left sleeve

stitch marker), 2 ch, 1 htr in same st, 1 htr in each of the next 19 (22) 24 (25) 26 sts, 1 dc in the next 6 sts and 1 dc in the first 6 sts on next back piece (this closes the slit in the neck), 1 htr in each of the next 20 (23) 25 (26) 27 sts, 6 (8) 8 (10) 11 ch (armhole), skip 36 (38) 41 (44) 46 sts (sleeve), 1 htr in each of the next 50 (54) 58 (62) 64 sts (front piece), 6 (8) 8 (10) 11 ch (armhole), skip 36 (38) 41 (44) 46 sts over (sleeve). Close round with 1 sl st in 1st htr through both loops (114 (128) 136 (146) 152 sts when counting ch from armhole). Turn and work the other way around.

Round 2: Ch 2, 1 htr in every st around, but work dc in 12 sts just below the vent on the back (114 (128) 136 (146) 152 sts). Turn.

Rep round 2 until a total of 6 rounds have been worked for the body. Then work straight with htr in every st in round back and forth until piece measures 18 (20) 22 (24) 26cm or desired length before peplum. Continue to make the peplum without breaking the yarn.

PEPLUM
On next round from RS, start on the peplum.
Round 1 (RS): ch 2, htr 1 in every st round through both loops to increase at every stitch (228 (256) 272 (292) 304 sts). Turn piece and work the opposite way.

Round 2: ch 2, 1 htr BLO in every st round (228 (256) 272 (292) 304 sts). Turn.

Rep round 2 until peplum measures 6 (6) 7 (7) 8cm. Finish with 1 sl st in every st from RS of peplum through both loops.
Break yarn and fasten off.

SLEEVE
Start by attaching the yarn in the middle of the armhole from RS. It is important to start from the right side for the rib pattern. Close each round with 1 sl st in 1st htr through both loops.

Round 1: Insert yarn in the middle of the armhole, work 2 ch, 1 htr in the same st, 1 htr in each of the next ch, work 1 htr around the htr on last row on yoke, rather than into it (in this case the htr is in the horizontal position), 1 htr in each of the 36 (38) 41 (44) 46 sts of the sleeve, work again 1 htr around the htr on last row of yoke, 1 htr in each of the remaining ch in armholes. Close round with 1 sl st in 1st htr through both loops. Turn and work the other way around (44 (48) 51 (56) 59 sts).

Round 2: ch 2, 1 htr in every st around – however, work 1 inc in each side where you worked around (rather than into) the htr on round 1 (42 (46) 49 (54) 57 sts). Close round with 1 sl st.
1st htr through both loops. Turn.

Round 3: Ch 2, htr 1, dec 1, htr 1 in remaining sts (41 (45) 48) 53 (56) sts). Close round with 1 sl st in 1st htr through both loops. Turn.

Rep round 3 with a single dc per round for a total of 7 (8) 9 (10) 11 rounds from armhole (total 37 (40) 42 (46) 48 sts and then finish the edge from RS with sl sts as follows: 1 sl st in every st through both loops.
Break yarn and finish off.
Work the other sleeve in the same way.

FINISHING

Sew on the button and weave in any remaining ends. Gently steam and press the blouse under a dry cloth.

Filippa's dress

This dress is simple and sweet, light and soft, and worked in double crochet and half treble. The design features a raglan neckline and a ruffle on the yoke. There is also a slit in the left back raglan line. The dress is worked from the neck down in one piece so that the length can be adjusted to suit each child.

Sizes
3 (6) 9 (12) 24 months

Measurements
Length: approx. 30 (34) 38 (40) 44cm
Circumference of bottom of dress: approx. 61 (72) 80 (86) 94cm

Yarn
Önling No 12, 55% wool, 45% cotton, 800 metres/115g
Colour: 32 light brown melange
Quantity: 1 (1) 2 (2) 2 balls

Other materials
1 mother-of-pearl button: approx. 1.5–2cm in diameter

Crochet hook
3mm

Tension
28 htr BLO x 20 rounds = 10 x 10cm

Note
Make sure that you work the very last st on a row; it can be difficult to find when working BLO.
Turning chains do not count towards the total stitch count.
Work dc rib on yoke with inc on every other row.
Mark raglan increases with stitch markers as explained in pattern.
Let stitch markers (preferably yarn in a contrasting colour) be carried forward for each row.
The first inc of the two worked around stitch marker is worked in st just above stitch marker.

Pattern
Work all sts BLO from 2nd row unless otherwise stated in pattern.

Tip

YOKE

Leave approx. 2 metres of yarn hanging at beg, which you will use to work sl sts etc. in neckline. Work sl sts as soon as you can to avoid having the yarn hanging during the rest of the work. Work 1 sl st in every st from RS with long end from cast-on, work 5 ch for buttonhole loop and fasten with 1 sl st a little further down slit. Work with sl sts around the edge of the slit.

Work 61 (67) 75 (81) 83 ch.

Row 1 (RS): 1 dc in 2nd ch from hook, 1 dc in every ch (60 (66) 74 (80) 82 sts). Turn.

Place stitch markers on RS of piece to keep track as you work.

Row 2: ch 1, 2 dc in 1st st (inc), 8 (9) 11 (11) 11 dc (shoulder), inc 1, PM, inc 1, 18 (20) 22 (25) 26 dc (front piece), inc 1, PM, inc 1, 8 (9) 11 (11) 11 dc (shoulder), inc 1, PM, inc 1, 18 (20) 22 (25) 26 dc (back), 2 dc in last st (inc) (total 68 (74) 82 (88) 90 sts). Turn.

Row 3: ch 1, dc 1 in each st (total 68 (74) 82 (88) 90 sts). Turn.

Row 4: Rep row 2, without raglan inc, as described, leaving stitch markers to mark the increases (76 (82) 90 (96) 98 sts).

Row 5: Rep row 3 without raglan ch (76 (82) 90 (96) 98 sts).

Rep rows 4 and 5 until a total of 10 (12) 14 (14) 16 rows have been increased. Finish yoke with a row 4. There are 140 (162) 186 (192) 210 sts in total on yoke.

BODY

Now continue on the bottom part of dress in half treble rib – over sts on back and front piece – as follows:

Round 1 (RS): ch 2, htr 1 (remember to work BLO) in 40 (46) 52 (55) 60 sts on back, ch 6 (8) 8 (10) 11 (armholes), skip shoulder 30 (35) 41 (41) 45 sts, work htr again in 40 (46) 52 (55) 60 sts (front), ch 6 (8) 8 (10) 11 (armholes), skip shoulder 30 (35) 41 (41) 45 sts. Work 1 sl st in 1st htr through both loops to form a ring (92 (108) 120 (130) 142 sts). Turn and work the other way round.

Round 2 (WS): 2 ch, 1 inc in every st; however, do not work an inc in the ch of the armhole, just 1 htr in every ch (172 (200) 224 (240) 262 sts). Turn.

Round 3 (RS): ch 2, 1 htr (BLO) in every st in the round (172 (200) 224 (240) 262 sts). Turn.

Rep round 3 alternately from RS and WS until piece measures 28 (32) 36 (37) 41cm or desired length.

Finish dress at hem with dc rib (pattern as on dress yoke): 8 (8) 8 (10) 10 rounds.
Finally finish the edge from RS with 1 sl st in every st through both loops.
Break yarn, finish off and fasten ends.

FLOUNCE

Work a flounce in htr rib on yoke. Start on RS at back of bottom of raglan slit, and let the flounce follow the row next to the shoulders. Let the neckline point downwards so that you work in the right direction, from the top down.

Tip

There are many yarn alternatives for this dress. Yarns that I use in the book, with a knitting tension of 27–28 htr and 20 rows = 10 x 10cm are suitable.

Round 1 (RS): slip yarn to any place behind on row, work 2 ch, inc 1 in every st all the way around in FLO (the free front stitches from the same sts in which the back and front piece are worked on – BLO). On shoulder 30 (35) 41 (41) 45 sts you may work through both stitch chains. Close round with 1 sl st in 1st htr through both loops (280 (324) 372 (384) 420 sts). Turn and work the opposite way.

Round 2: ch 2, 1 htr in every st BLO. Close round with 1 sl st in 1st htr through both loops. Turn.

Rep round 2 until there are a total of 3 (3) 3 (4) 4 rounds on flounce.
Finish from RS by working 1 sl st in every st through both loops.
Break yarn and fasten off.

FINISHING

Work in the last ends.
Sew a button on the yoke.
Gently steam and press the dress under a dry cloth.

Otto's cardigan

This long, jacket-like cardigan has a raglan neckline and pockets that can be left out if preferred. The design is worked in one piece with double crochet and half treble crochet. Approx. 5cm extra length is included for a turn on the sleeve. The cardigan is worked in Merilin from Isager.

Sizes
3 (6) 12 (24) months

Measurements
Width: approx. 48 (52) 56 (58)cm
Length: approx. 30 (35) 40 (40)cm

Yarn
Isager Merilin, 80% wool and 20% linen,
208 metres/50g
Colour: 47 blue/grey
Quantity: 150 (200) 200 (250)g

Other materials
6 (7) 8 (8) buttons: 1.5cm in diameter

Crochet hooks
3mm and 3.5mm

Tension
26 htr BLO x 20 rows = 10 x 10cm

Note
Make sure that you work the very last st on a row; it can be difficult to find when working BLO.

Turning chains are not counted in the total stitch count.
Mark raglan with stitch markers as explained in pattern.
Let the stitch markers (preferably yarn in a contrasting colour) be carried forward for each row.
The first inc of the two worked around the stitch marker is worked in st just above the stitch marker.

Pattern
Work all sts BLO from row 2 unless otherwise stated in pattern.

Front button band
Work dc rib over 8 sts on each side of cardigan all the way down from neck edge.

Buttonholes
Work until 5 sts remain, ch 2, skip 2 sts and work 1 dc in the last 3 sts. On the next row work 2 dc in ch-loop. Buttonholes are worked every 12 rows.

NECK RIB

Work 11 ch with 3mm hook.
Row 1: 1 dc in 2nd ch from hook, and in the next 9 ch (10 sts). Turn.

Row 2: ch 1, dc 1 in BLO to end (10).

Rep row 2 until there are 76 (86) 98 (106) rows in total. Make a buttonhole on row 74 (84) 96 (104) (this is the 3rd last row of rib) as follows: 4 dc, ch 2, skip 2 sts, 4 dc. On next row work 2 dc in ch-loop.

Finish the neck dc rib with a sl st in each of the 10 sts through both loops. Do not break yarn. Also work sl sts at other end of rib. Feel free to use the yarn end from the start – it gives a neat finish to the neck edge.

Change to 3.5mm hook and continue along the side of the neck rib as follows:

Row 1 (RS): ch 1, work 1 st for every row on rib divided by 8 dc, 60 (70) 82 (90) htr, 8 dc (total 76 (86) 98 (106) sts). Turn.

Row 2 (WS): remember to work BLO. 1 ch, 8 dc, 8 (8) 10 (12) htr (right front piece), PM, 10 (14) 16 (17) htr (sleeve), PM, 24 (26) 30 (32) htr (back), PM, 10 (14) 16 (17) sts (sleeve), PM, 8 (8) 10 (12) htr, 8 dc (left front piece) (total 76 (86) 98 (106) sts). Turn.

Row 3: ch 1, dc 8, htr 7 (7) 9 (11), inc 1, slip marker, inc 1, 8 (12) 14 (15) htr, inc 1, slip marker, inc 1, 22 (24) 28 (30) htr, inc 1, slip marker, inc 1, 8 (12) 14 (15) htr, inc 1, slip marker, inc 1, 7 (7) 9 (11) htr, 8 dc (total 84 (94) 106 (114) sts). Turn.

Row 4: ch 1, dc 8, htr 8 (8) 10 (12), inc 1, slip marker, inc 1, 10 (14) 16 (17) htr, inc 1, slip marker, inc 1, 24 (26) 30 (32) htr, inc 1, slip marker, inc 1, 10 (14) 16 (17) htr, inc 1, slip marker, inc 1, 8 (8) 10 (12) htr, 8 dc incl. a buttonhole (total 92 (102) 114 (122) sts).

Turn. Then work buttonholes every 12 rows.

Rep inc on every row a total of 15 (16) 17 (18) times on yoke. A total of 17 (18) 19 (20) rows have been worked. There is now a total of 196 (214) 234 (250) sts divided into 31 (32) 35 (38) sts (front piece), 40 (46) 50 (53) sts (sleeve), 54 (58) 64 (68) sts (back), 40 (46) 50 (53) sts (sleeve), 31 (32) 35 (38) sts front piece. Do not break yarn.

BODY

Now continue to work on back and front pieces.

Next row: ch 1, dc 8, 23 (24) 27 (30) htr (front piece), 6 (8) 8 (10) ch (armhole), skip 40 (46) 50 (53) sts (sleeve), 1 htr in the next 54 (58) 64 (68) sts (back), 6 (8) 8 (10) ch (armhole), skip 40 (46) 50 (53) sts over (sleeve), 23 (24) 27 (30) htr (front piece), 8 dc (total 128 (138) 150 (164) sts). Turn.

Next row: ch 1, dc 8, 112 (122) 134 (148) htr, 8 dc (total 128 (138) 150 (164) sts). Turn.

If you want to have pockets on the sweater, work at the same time as described under 'Pockets'.

NOTE: Pockets must be worked approx. 5–6cm before full length of sweater.

Rep last row straight until piece measures 30 (35) 40 (40)cm. Remember the buttonholes.

On the last row of the cardigan, work 12 (14) 18 (22) evenly spaced decs (not in button bands) (116 (124) 132 (142) sts).

Finish the edge of 1 sl st (not too tight) in every st through both loops.
Break yarn and finish off.

POCKETS

Work 2 pocket edges in form of dc rib (as for neck edge) over 10 sts and work 16 (18) 20 (22) rows.

Work 1 sl st in each of the 10 sts at both ends of pocket edge. Leave a yarn end of approx. 20cm at both ends to sew the dc rib to the cardigan.

Break the yarn.

When you have worked to the 6th row after the 5th (6th) row 7th (7th) buttonhole on body (this is about 5–6cm before full length of cardigan), work pocket edges onto cardigan on next row from RS as follows:

Next row (RS): ch 1, 8 dc, 4 htr, 1 htr in each row across dc rib/pocket edge (i.e. 16 (18) 20 (22) htr), at the same time skip 16 (18) 20 (22) sts on body piece itself, then 1 htr in every st on body until 28 (30) 32 (34) sts remain. Fasten the other pocket edge as just described and skip again 16 (18) 20 (22) sts on body piece, 4 htr, 8 dc (128 (138) 150 (164) sts in total).

At the same time work on cardigan as described under body.

Work an inside pocket piece on both sides over the 16 (18) 20 (22) sts on body piece that were skipped when pocket edge was worked in place. It does not matter which side you start on.

Work 10 rows dc through both loops back and forth with 3.5mm crochet hook or until pocket measures approx. 5cm.

Work a similar pocket piece on the other side of the cardigan.

On the penultimate row of the cardigan, work the pocket pieces tog with the rest of the cardigan so that the pockets are closed at the bottom. On 3rd row after 6th (7th) 8th (8th) buttonhole, attach the bottom of the pocket pieces as follows:

Next row (RS): ch 1, 8 dc, 4 htr, work the next 16 (18) 20 (22) sts tog 2 by 2 with 16 (18) 20 (22) sts (still in BLO on cardigan but through both loops on pocket piece) through both layers, 1 htr in every st until 28 (30) 32 (34) sts remain. Fasten the second pocket piece in the same way, 4 htr and 8 dc.

SLEEVE

Start in the middle of armhole. Remember to fit the pattern so that you work BLO from both RS and WS.

Round 1: start from RS on size 3 and 12 months, from WS on size 6 and 24 months. Cast on yarn, work 2 ch, 1 htr in same st, 1 htr in each of next ch, work 1 htr around htr on last row on yoke, rather than into it (in this case the htr is in the horizontal position), 1 htr in each of sleeve's 40 (46) 50 (53) sts, work again 1 htr around htr on last row on yoke, 1 htr in each of the last ch in armhole. Close round with 1 sl st. 1st htr through both loops (48 (56) 60 (65 sts). Turn and work the other way around.

Round 2: ch 2, 1 htr in every st in the round. Crochet an increase on each side where you worked around (rather than into) the htr in round 1. Close round with 1 sl st in 1st htr through both loops (46 (54) 58 (63) sts). Turn.

Round 3: Ch 2, 1 htr in every st in the round. Close round with 1 sl st in 1st htr through both loops (46 (54) 58 (63) sts). Turn.

Rep round 3. Make sure to work a single dec when sleeve measures 5 and 15cm (44 (52) 56 (61) sts). When sleeve measures approximately 23 (28) 31 (34) cm from armhole – or desired length – on last round work 8 (8) 10 (10) evenly spaced decs (36 (44) 46 (51) sts).

Tip

Manna's moccasins and Karl Viggo's trousers co-ordinate well with the cardigan.

Now finish the edge from RS: 1 sl st (not too tight) in every st through both loops.
Break yarn and fasten off.
Work the other sleeve the same way.

FINISHING
Weave in any remaining ends.
Sew on buttons with the yarn you are working in. Sew the pocket pieces to the WS, and sew the ribbed edges of the pockets to the RS of the sweater with discreet stitches.
Gently steam and press the cardigan under a dry cloth.

Olga's sweater

*Olga's sweater is worked top down in one piece, so there are no uncomfortable seams
for the baby to lie on. There is a button on the slit at the neck, so the sweater is easy
to put on and take off. There is raglan shaping on the yoke. I have worked with two
strands of Isager Alpaca 1 in a dip-dye colourway. The sweater features double crochet
and half treble rib, so it is relatively elastic.*

Sizes
6 (9) 12 (24) months

Measurements
Chest width: approx. 48 (52) 56 (60)cm
Length: approx. 28 (30) 34 (37)cm

Yarn
Isager Alpaca 1, 100% alpaca, 400
metres/50g
Colours: 16 sea green, 47 blue-grey, 11 light
blue, 54 petrol blue, black, 46 light green,
light grey 3S
Quantity: 50g of each colour – 7 colours in
total – is enough for all sizes.
Size 9 months, for example, weighs 175g.

Other materials
1 mother-of-pearl button: 1.5cm in diameter

Crochet hooks
3mm and 3.5mm

Tension
Worked in two strands Alpaca 1
26 htr BLO x 20 rows = 10 x 10cm

Note
Work in double yarn, continuously changing
one thread according to the colour list.
There are some ends to fasten because of the
dip-dye colour change. You can weave in
two strands at a time.
Make sure you work the very last st on a
row; it can be hard to find when working
BLO.
Turning chains are not counted in the total
stitch count.
Mark raglan increases with stitch markers as
explained in pattern.
Let the stitch markers (preferably yarn in a
contrasting colour) be carried forward for
each row.
The first of the two increases worked around
the stitch marker is worked in st just above
the stitch marker.
The join on rounds is placed mid-back.

Pattern
All sts are worked BLO from row 2 unless
otherwise stated in pattern.

*This alternative colourway is
worked in peach and pink.
See the tip on page 62.*

Dip-dye colour list

Rib is worked in two strands of sea green.
1st colour change on 3rd row.
Then change colour every 4th row/round.
1st change: change one strand of sea green yarn to black.
2nd change: change one strand of sea green yarn to black.
3rd change: change one strand of black yarn to grey.
4th change: change one strand of black yarn to grey.
5th change: change one strand of grey yarn to blue-grey.
6th change: change one strand of grey yarn to blue-grey.
7th change: change one strand of blue-grey yarn to light blue.
8th change: change one strand of blue-grey yarn to light blue.
9th change: change one strand of light blue yarn to petrol blue.
10th change: change one strand of light blue yarn to petrol blue.
11th change: change one strand of petrol blue yarn to light green.
12th change: change one strand of petrol blue yarn to light green.
13th change: change one strand of light green yarn to sea green.
14th change: change one strand of light green yarn to sea green.
Rep colour changes 1 to 14 until piece is desired length.

Tip

There are many possibilities for colour combinations in Isager Alpaca 1. For the peach and pink shades of the sweater on page 61 (size 12 months) approx. 100g yarn in each of the colours pink and peach are used. Start by working about one third with two strands of peach, then one strand of pink and peach, and work at the bottom with two strands of pink.

YOKE

Start with a dc rib on the neckline. Work 11 ch with two strands sea green alpaca 1 and 3mm crochet hook.

Row 1: 1 dc in 2nd ch from hook and in the next 9 ch (10 sts in total). Turn.
Row 2: ch 1, dc 1 in BLO row (10 sts). Turn.

Rep row 2. Work a buttonhole in the 3rd last row as follows: Work 4 dc, ch 2, skip 2 sts, 4 dc. On next row work 2 dc in ch-loop. Otherwise work straight until a total of 76 (86) 98 (106) rows have been worked. Finish rib with 1 sl st in every st through both loops. Do not break yarn.

Also work sl sts at other end of rib. Feel free to use the yarn end from the beginning – it gives a neat finish to the neck edge.

Change to 3.5mm hook.

Row 1 (RS): ch 2, then work 1 htr for every row along rib (76 (86) 98 (106) sts in total). Turn.

Row 2 (WS): ch 2, 16 (16) 18 (20) htr (left back piece), PM, 10 (14) 16 (17) htr (sleeve), PM, 24 (26) 30 (32) sts (front piece), PM, 10 (14) 16 (17) htr (sleeve), PM, 16 (16) 18 (20) sts (right back piece) (76 (86) 98 (106) sts). Turn.

Row 3 (RS): Change a yarn strand, following the dip-dye colour list. 2 ch, 15 (15) 17 (19) htr, inc 1, slip marker, inc 1, 8 (12) 14 (15) htr, inc 1, slip marker, inc 1, 22 (24) 28 (30) htr, inc 1, slip marker, inc 1, 8 (12) 14 (15) htr, inc 1, slip marker, inc 1, 15 (15) 17 (19) htr (total 84 (94) 106 (114) sts). Turn. Follow the colour chart for the rest of the piece. Yarn is broken for each colour change.

Row 4 (WS): ch 2, 16 (16) 18 (20) htr, inc 1, slip marker, inc 1, 10 (14) 16 (17) htr, inc 1, slip marker, inc 1, 24 (26) 30 (32) htr, inc 1, slip marker, inc 1, 10 (14) 16 (17) htr, inc 1, slip marker, inc 1, 16 (16) 18 (20) htr (total 92 (102) 114 (122) sts). Turn.

Rep raglan increases, as described, on every row. When a total of 8 rows have been worked from dc rib, close piece to form a ring (124 (134) 146 (154) sts).

Row 9 (RS): ch 2, close neck slit by working first 5 sts and last 5 sts. Place 5 sts from right side on top of 5 sts from left side – this should fit with the overlap created when closing with a button on the neck. Work sts tog 2 by 2 through both layers with htr through both loops. Continue with hdc, and raglan increases in the round. Close round with 1 sl st in 1st htr. Piece is now closed to a ring (127 (137) 149 (157) sts in total).

Break yarn.
Turn and work the opposite way round.

Round 10 (WS): Slip yarn to centre of back, ch 2, work 1 htr in same st, 19 (19) 21 (23) htr, inc 1, slip marker, inc 1, 22 (26) 28 (29) htr, inc 1, slip marker, inc 1, (36 (38) 42 (44) sts, inc 1, slip marker, inc 1, 22 (26) 28 (29) htr, inc 1, slip marker, inc 1, 19 (19) 21 (23) htr. Close round with 1 sl st in 1st htr. (135 (145) 157 (165) sts). Turn.

Rep raglan increases as described on each round until a total of 15 (16) 17 (18) increase rounds have been worked – 17 (18) 19 (20) rows/rounds are worked on yoke. There are 191 (209) 229 (245) sts on piece divided into

Tip

If necessary, work pockets on front of sweater. Pockets are described for Otto's cardigan, p. 57.

29 (30) 33 (36) sts (back), 40 (46) 50 (53) sts (sleeve), 54 (58) 64 (68) sts (front piece), 40 (46) 50 (53) sts (sleeve), 28 (29) 32 (35) sts (back).

BODY

Continue working on body. First work a 1st round with htr, dividing sts as follows. The sleeves and body can then be finished separately.

Round 1: Continue from RS on size 6 months and 12 months, from WS on size 9 and 24 months. Ch 2, 1 htr in first RS: 28 (29) 32 (35) sts (back) WS: 29 (30) 33 (36) sts (back) 6 (8) 8 (8) ch (armholes), skip 40 (46) 50 (53) sts (sleeve), 1 htr in next 54 (58) 64 (68) sts (front piece), work 6 (8) 8 (8) ch (armholes), skip 40 (46) 50 (53) sts (sleeve), work htr in last RS: 29 (30) 33 (36) sts/WS: 28 (29) 32 (35) sts (back). There are 123 (133) 145 (155) sts in total on body. Turn and work the other way around.

Round 2: 2 ch, 1 htr in every st. 123 (133) 145 (155) sts. Turn.

Rep round 2 straight with colour change until piece measures 27 (29) 33 (36)cm or desired length.

On last round work 12 (14) 18 (22) decs evenly (total 111 (119) 127 (133) sts).

Finish with an edge of 1 sl st (not too tight) in every st through both loops.
Break yarn and fasten off.

SLEEVE

Start in the middle of armhole. Pattern with htr rib should fit, so that you work BLO from the RS.
Round 1: Work from RS on size 6 months and 12 months, from WS on size 9 months and 24 months. Cast on yarn with 2 ch, work 1 htr in same st, 1 htr in each of the next ch, work 1 htr around htr on last row on yoke, rather than into it (in this case the htr is in the horizontal position), 1 htr in each of sleeve 40 (46) 50 (53) sts, work again 1 htr around the htr on last row on yoke, 1 htr in each of the last ch in armhole. Close round with 1 sl st in 1st htr through both loops (48 (56) 60 (65 sts). Turn and work the opposite way.

Round 2: ch 2, 1 htr (BLO) in every st in the round. Work an increase on each side where you worked around (rather than into) the htr in round 1. Close round with 1 sl st in 1st htr through both loops (46 (54) 58 (63) sts). Turn.

Round 3: ch 2, 1 htr in every st in the round (46 (54) 58 (63) sts). Turn.

Rep round 3. Make sure to work a dec when sleeve measures 5 and 15cm (44 (52) 56 (61) sts). When sleeve measures approximately 23 (28) 31 (34)cm from armhole – or desired length – on last round work 8 (8) 10 (10) evenly spaced decs (36 (44) 46 (51) sts in total).

Approx. 5cm extra length is included for a turn on sleeve. The fold can be omitted.

Finally, finish the edge from RS: 1 sl st (not too tight) in every st through both loops.
Break yarn and fasten off.
Work the other sleeve the same way.

FINISHING

Weave in all ends. Sew on a button.
Gently steam and press sweater under a dry cloth.
If desired, attach a length of elastic to the bottom of the sweater. The elastic is inserted and pulled out between sts on the second to last round.

Ester's cardigan

Ester's cardigan is a nice basic cardigan, which has an optional flounce on the round yoke. The cardigan is worked in one piece from top to bottom. The whole cardigan is worked in half treble crochet.

Size
6 (12) 18 (24) months

Measurements
Chest width: 50 (55) 65 (65)cm. Wider at the bottom after neckline.
Length: approx. 25 (30) 33 (36)cm

Yarn
Onion Organic Cotton, 100% organic cotton, 155 metres/50g
Colour: light pink 150
Quantity: 200 (200) 250 (250)g

Other materials
6 (7) 7 (8) pearl or horn buttons: 1.5–2cm in diameter

Crochet hook
3.5mm

Tension
23 htr BLO x 15 rows = 10 x 10cm

Note
Make sure you work the very last st on a row; it can be hard to find when working BLO.
Turning chains are not counted in total stitch count.
Place a stitch marker on RS of piece.
Make sure increases are evenly spaced on yoke and not just above each other from row to row.

Pattern
All sts are worked BLO from row 2 unless otherwise stated in pattern.

Buttonholes
Work htr until 4 sts remain on row, then ch 1, skip 1 st and work 1 htr in last 3 sts. On next row work 1 htr in ch-space. Buttonhole is worked every 6th row.

A pink cardigan, size 18 months, with flounce.

YOKE

Leave approx. 2 metres of yarn hanging at beg, which you will need to work the neckline. Work sl st as soon as you can. You then avoid having the yarn hanging during the rest of the work. Work 1 sl st in every st from RS with the long end from cast-on.

Work 62 (68) 76 (80) ch.

Row 1 (RS): 1 htr in 3rd ch from hook, 1 htr in every subsequent ch (60 (66) 74 (78) sts total). Turn.

Row 2 (WS): ch 2, 1 htr (remember to work BLO) in every st, at the same time work 8 incs evenly spaced and a buttonhole at the end of row (68 (74) 82 (86) sts). Turn.

Row 3 (RS): ch 2, 1 htr in every st, at the same time work 8 incs evenly spaced (76 (82) 90 (94) sts). Turn.

Row 4 (WS): ch 2, htr 1 in each st, at the same time work 8 incs evenly spaced (84 (90) 98 (102) sts) Turn.

Rep incs, increasing the number of stitches by 8 sts on every row 10 (12) 14 (14) times in total. There are a total of 11 (13) 15 (15) rows and 140 (162) 186 (190) sts on piece.

Do not break the yarn – continue working on sleeves and body separately.

BODY

Now work on front and back piece, dividing the piece as follows:
21 (24) 27 (29) sts (front piece), 30 (35) 41 (40) sts (sleeve), 38 (44) 50 (52) sts (back piece), 30 (35) 41 (40) sts (sleeve) and 21 (24) 27 (29) sts (front piece).

Row 1 (WS): 2 ch, 1 htr in the first 21 (24) 27 (29) sts, skip 30 (35) 41 (40) sts, work 4 (6) 8 (10) ch (armhole), 1 htr in each of next 38 (44) 50 (52) sts, skip 30 (35) 41 (40) sts, work 4 (6) 8 (10) ch (armholes), 1 htr in the last 21 (24) 27 (29) sts (88 (104) 120 (130) st.

Row 2 (RS): ch 2, 1 htr in every st, at the same time work 15 (20) 25 (30) incs evenly (103 (124) 145 (160) sts). Turn.

Row 3 (WS): ch 2, 1 htr in every st (103 (124) 145 (160) sts). Turn.

Rep row 3 until cardigan measures approximately 25 (30) 33 (36)cm or desired length. Remember to work buttonholes. Work 8 (9) 10 (11) decs evenly on last row from WS (total 95 (115) 135 (149) sts).
Finish with an edge of 1 sl st in every st through both loops from RS.
Break yarn and fasten ends.

SLEEVES

Work sleeves with htr rib on every round. Begin by attaching yarn to centre of sleeve yoke. Make sure to start from WS, as rib pattern must fit, by working BLO from the right side.

Round 1 (WS): join yarn in the middle of armhole with 2 ch, 1 htr in the same st, then 1 htr in each of the next ch, work 1 htr around the htr on last row of yoke, rather than into it (in this case the htr is in the horizontal position), work 1 htr in each of the 30 (35) 41 (40) sts of sleeve, work again 1 htr around the htr on last row on yoke, and finish with 1 htr in each of the last ch in armhole. Close round with a sl st in 1st htr through both loops (36 (43) 51 (52) sts).

A blue cardigan, size 24 months, without flounce.

Tip

The blue sweater with horn buttons is crocheted without a flounce on the yoke.

If you would like a smaller flounce, just work the 1st row and the chain stitch edge.

Turn and work the opposite way around.

Round 2 (RS): 2 ch, 1 htr in every st, also work 1 dec in each side of sleeve where you worked around (rather than into) the htr in round 1. Close round with 1 sl st in 1st htr (34 (41) 49 (50) sts).

Round 3: Ch 2, 1 htr in every st. Close round with 1 sl st in 1st htr (34 (41) 49 (50) sts).

Work straight until sleeve measures 17 (20) 24 (26)cm from armhole or desired length. You can work an extra length of 5cm and make a small turn-up on sleeve.
Work 4 (5) 6 (6) decs from WS on last round (total 30 (36) 43 (44) sts). Then work a round with 1 sl st in every st through both loops from RS.
Break yarn and finish off.
Work the other sleeve the same way.

FLOUNCE

Work a flounce of htr rib over 3 (3) 4 (4) rows on yoke.

Join yarn in first st (in free stitch space) by counting 10, 12 or 14 rows from beginning of neckline (yoke hangs down while working flounce from top down).

Row 1 (RS): ch 2, htr 2 in every st all around (FLO). Do not work in the last 4 sts – on the side where the buttons are sewn on – there should be room for overlap when the cardigan is buttoned (total 272 (316) 364 (372) sts). Turn.

Row 2: ch 2, 1 htr BLO in every st (272 (316) 364 (372) sts). Turn.

Rep row 2 until a total of 3 (3) 4 (4) rows have been worked on flounce.
Finish flounce with sl st in every st around. Break yarn and fasten ends.

FINISHING

Sew on buttons and weave in the last ends.

Gently steam and press sweater under a dry cloth.

Erik's jacket

This sweater is constructed like Ester's sweater, but it is worked without a flounce, in three colours and on a 4mm hook.

Size
6 (12) 24 months

Measurements
Ample width across the chest. Wider on body after increases.
Length: approx. 30 (34) 37cm

Yarn
Önling No 14, 78% cotton and 22% linen,
125 metres/50g
Colour A dark linen 4
Colour B light linen 668
Colour C dark grey 2
Quantity: 100g of each colour

Other materials
Pearl buttons: 2cm in diameter (number depends on your spacing)

Crochet hook
4mm

Tension
21 htr BLO x 12 rows = 10 x 10cm

Note
Make sure that you work the very last st on a row; it can be difficult to find when working BLO.
Turning chains are not counted in total stitch count.
Place a stitch marker on RS of piece.
Make sure increases are evenly spaced on yoke and not just above each other from row to row.

Pattern
All sts are worked BLO from row 2 unless otherwise stated in pattern.

Buttonholes
Work htr until 4 sts remain on row, then ch 1, skip 1 st and work 1 htr in the last 3 sts. Rep on every 4th row.

Jacket worked in Önling no 14.

YOKE

Start with colour A.
Leave approx. 2 metres yarn hanging at the beginning, which you will use to work the sl st edge.
Neckline: Work the sl st edge as soon as you can, then you can avoid having the yarn hanging during the rest of the work. With the long end from the cast-on, work 1 sl st in every st from RS.

Work 67 (77) 81 ch.

Row 1 (RS): 1 htr in 3rd ch from hook, 1 htr in every subsequent ch (65 (75) 79 sts total). Turn.

Row 2: ch 2, 1 htr (remember to work BLO) in every st, at the same time work 8 incs evenly spaced, and work a buttonhole at the end of row (73 (83) (87) sts). Turn.

Row 3: ch 2, 1 htr in every st, work 8 incs evenly at the same time (81 (91) 95 sts). Turn.

Row 4: ch 2, htr 1 in every st, work 8 incs evenly at the same time (89 (100) 103 sts). Turn.

Rep increases, increasing the number of stitches by 8 sts on every row 12 (14) 16 times in total. There is a total of 13 (15) 17 rows and 161 (187) 207 sts in total on piece.

Do not break the yarn.

BODY

Now work on front and back piece, dividing the piece as follows, adding a stitch marker after each section, if desired:

23 (26) 29 sts (front piece), 34 (41) 45 sts (sleeve), 44 (50) 56 sts (back), 34 (41) 45 sts (sleeve) and 26 (29) 32 sts (front piece).

Tip

The buttons are tight, so you can work buttonholes on every 6th row instead.

Row 1 (WS): ch 2, 1 htr in first 23 (26) 29 sts, skip 34 (41) 45 sts, work 4 (5) 6 ch (armholes), 1 htr in each of next 44 (50) 56 sts, skip 34 (41) 45 sts, work 4 (5) 6 ch (armholes), 1 htr in last 26 (29) 32 sts (total 101 (115) 129 sts). Turn.

Row 2 (RS): ch 2, *1 htr, inc 1*, rep from * to * to end (do not increase in ch in armhole) (148 (168) 188 sts). Turn.

Row 3: ch 2, 1 htr in each st (148 (168) 188 sts). Turn.

Rep row 3 and work back and forth until jacket measures 25 (30) 36cm in total – or to desired length.
Change to colour B when 6 rows have been worked on body. Change to colour C when 15 rows have been worked on body. Work to full length of garment with colour C.
Remember to work buttonholes.
Work 8 (9) 10 decs evenly on last row (140 (159) 178 sts).
Finish with an edge of 1 sl st through both loops in every st from RS.
Break yarn, finish off and fasten ends.

SLEEVES

Work sleeves with htr rib on every round.
Start by attaching yarn to the middle of sleeve yoke. Remember that the pattern must fit so that you work BLO from the RS.
Work colour change as on body.

Round 1 (WS): put colour A in the middle of armhole, work 2 ch, 1 htr in the same st, then 1 htr in each of the next ch, work 1 htr around the htr on last row on yoke, rather than into it (in this case the htr is in the horizontal position), work 1 htr in each of the 34 (41) 45 sts of sleeve, work again 1 htr around the htr on last row on yoke, and finish with 1 htr in each of the last ch in armhole. Close round with 1 sl st in 1st htr through both loops (40 (48) 53 sts). Turn and work the other way round.

Round 2 (RS): 2 ch, 1 htr in every st, also work 1 dec in each side of sleeve where you worked around (rather than into) the htr in round 1. Close round with 1 sl st in 1st htr through both loops (38 (46) 51 sts). Turn.

Round 3: Ch 2, 1 htr in every st. Close round with 1 sl st in 1st htr through both loops (38 (46) 51 sts). Turn.

Continue working until sleeve measures 20 (24) 28cm from armhole – or to desired length. You can also work extra length of 5cm and make a turn-up on the sleeve.
On last round work 5 (6) 7 decs (total 33 (40) 44 sts).
Then work one round with sl sts in every st from RS.
Break yarn and finish off.
Work the other sleeve the same way.

FINISHING

Sew on buttons with the colour of yarn you are working in. Gently steam and press the sweater under a dry cloth.

Tip

You can crochet a flounce on the yoke, as on Ester's cardigan (see p. 70).

Anton's nappy pants

The nappy pants are worked from the rib at the waist down in one piece so there are no uncomfortable seams for the baby to lie on. You can choose to crochet the pants with or without ruffles. The pattern consists of double crochet and half treble crochet. I have crocheted the nappy pants in the different yarn types indicated in the pattern, so choose a colour you prefer; there are many nice ones available.

Sizes
3 (6) 12 (24) months

Measurements
Length: approx. 20 (23) 26 (29)cm
Waist: approx. 36 (41) 44 (46)cm

Yarn
Gepard CottonWool 3 Organic, 50% wool and 50% cotton, 230 metres/50g
or: Gepard My Fine Wool, 100% superfine merino, 233 metres/50g
or: Sandnes Sunday, 100% merino, 235 metres/50g

Quantity: 100 (100) 100 (150)g (applies to all three yarn options)

Other materials
Elastic: 60–70cm, approx. 1.5cm wide

Crochet hooks
2.5mm and 3mm

Tension
27–28 htr BLO x 20 rows = 10 x 10cm

Note
Turning chains do not count in the total number of stitches.
Divide 10 dc on each side of pants later and continue as rib in leg openings.
Let the stitch markers (preferably yarn) be carried forward round by round so that the 10 dc in each side are just above each other.

Pattern
All sts are worked BLO from 2nd row unless otherwise stated in pattern.

Anton's nappy pants worked in Önling No 11, which matches Milla's blouse on p. 42.

RIB

Work 11 ch with 2.5mm hook.

Row 1 (RS): 1 dc in 2nd ch from hook, 1 dc in every st (10 sts). Turn.

Row 2: ch 1, dc in every ch (10 sts). Turn.

Rep row 2 until there are 100 (114) 122 (126) rows dc-rib in total.
Then work rib together with sl sts RS to RS to form a ring by working sts tog 2 by 2 through both layers.
Do not break yarn.

PANTS

Change to 3mm hook.

Round 1 (RS): 3 ch, 100 (114) 122 (126) tr in the round along rib edge. Close round with 1 sl st in 1st tr through both loops (100 (114) 122 (126) sts).

Round 1 was worked in tr because there should be room to pull a length of elastic through sts on this round.

Divide into front and back piece with placement of stitch markers and work BLO from round 2.

Round 2 (RS again): ch 1, dc 1 (remember BLO from now on) in next 5 sts, PM, 40 (47) 51 (53) hdc, PM, dc 1 in next 5 sts, PM. These first 50 (57) 61 (63) sts are the back piece. If you like, put a stitch marker on the RS of the back piece. Continue crocheting for 2 rounds: dc 1 in next 40 (47) 51 (53) hdc, PM, dc 1 in next 5 st. Close round with 1 sl st in 1st dc through both loops. These 50 (57) 61 (63) sts are front piece (total 100 (114) 122 (126) sts). Turn and work the other way around.

Round 3 (WS): ch 1, dc 5, slip marker, 40 (47) 51 (53) htr (front piece), slip marker, 5 dc, slip

Tip

Anton's nappy pants in Sandnes Sunday yarn are shown together with Manna's moccasins and Anton's winter blouse on pp. 126 and 127.

marker, 5 dc, slip marker, 40 (47) 51 (53) htr (back piece), slip marker, 5 dc. Close round with 1 sl st in 1st dc through both loops (100 (114) 122 (126) sts in total). Turn.

Round 4 (RS): ch 1, dc 5, 40 (47) 51 (53) htr (back piece), slip marker, 5 dc, slip marker, 5 dc, slip marker, 40 (47) 51 (53) htr (front piece), slip marker, 5 dc. Close round with 1 sl st in 1st dc through both loops (100 (114) 122 (126) sts in total). Turn.

Rep rounds 3 and 4 until a total of 20 (24) 26 (28) rounds from rib. Finish with a round from WS.

Round 21 (25) 27 (29) (RS): ch 1, dc 5, 40 (47) 51 (53) htr, 5 dc (back piece), slip marker, 15 dc, slip marker, 20 (27) 31 (33) htr, slip marker, 15 dc (front piece). Close round with a sl st in 1st dc through both loops (100 (114) 122 (126) sts total). Turn.

Round 22 (26) 28 (30) (WS): ch 1, 15 dc, slip marker, 20 (27) 31 (33) htr, slip marker, 15 dc (front piece), PM, 5 dc, slip marker, 40 (47) 51 (53) htr, slip marker, 5 dc (back piece). Close round with 1 sl st in 1st dc through both loops (100 (114) 122 (126) sts total). Turn.

Rep the last 2 rounds a total of 3 times. There are 26 (30) 32 (34) rounds from rib.

Piece is now divided into front piece and back piece, as the pieces will be worked back and forth separately.

Tip

You can also crochet a ribbon to use instead of the waist
tie. Use the same yarn as for the nappy pants. Work approx.
180–200 ch and work 1 htr in 3rd ch, 1 sl st in each of the next
ch until last ch, 1 htr in last st.

Round 27 (31) 33 (35) (RS): ch 1, dc 5, 40 (47) 51 (53) htr, slip marker, 5 dc (back piece), 10 sl sts, ch 1 (to level with the next dc), 5 dc, slip marker, 20 (27) 31 (33) htr, slip marker, 5 dc (front piece), 10 sl sts. Close round with 1 sl st in 1st dc through both loops (100 (114) 122 (126) sts in total). Break yarn.
Turn piece and finish front section.

FRONT SECTION
Row 1 (WS): Skip 10 sts, join yarn, ch 1, dc 1 in same st and next 4 sts, slip marker, 2 htr tog (dec), 16 (23) 27 (29) htr, 2 htr tog (dec), PM, dc 1 in last 5 sts (28 (35) 39 (41) sts). Turn.

Row 2 (RS): ch 1, dc 5, slip marker, htr 2 tog (dec), htr 14 (21) 25 (27), htr 2 tog (dec), slip marker, dc 5 (26 (33) 37 (39) sts). Turn.

Rep rows 1 and 2 with 2 decs on each row. There are 2 sts fewer between dec from row to row. Work until 16 (19) 23 (23) sts remain on piece.
Then work 8 (8) 10 (10) rows straight as sts show, without decs.
Break yarn and finish off.

BACK SECTION
Row 1 (WS): slip yarn over 1st st on back section, ch 1, dc 1 in same st and next 4 sts, slip marker, 2 htr tog (inc), 36 (43) 47 (49) htr, 2 htr tog (inc), slip marker, 5 dc (48 (55) 59 (61) sts). Turn.

Row 2 (RS): ch 1, dc 5, slip marker, htr 2 tog (dec), htr 34 (41) 45 (47), htr 2 tog (dec), slip marker, dc 5 (46 (53) 57 (59) sts). Turn.

Rep rows 1 and 2 with 2 decs on each row until 16 (19) 23 (23) sts remain on piece – same number of sts as on front piece.

Turn WS outwards on piece and work front and back sections together RS tog by working 2 sts tog through both layers with 1 sl st. Break yarn and finish off.

RUFFLES (OPTIONAL)
You can work two flounces on the back piece in htr rib.
The first flounce is worked in line with row for beg of dec. Work from RS so that dc rib edge hangs down in lap, so that you can work in the right direction from top to bottom. Fold the back piece along the row in which the flounce is to be worked – this makes it easier to pick up a stitch with the hook. Do not work flounce in dc rib, i.e. do not work in the 5 outermost sts on each side.

Row 1 (RS): insert yarn in 6th st from edge, work 2 ch, 2 htr in every st along. Turn.

Row 2 (WS): ch 2, 1 htr (remember to work BLO from now on) in every st along. Turn.

Row 3 (RS): ch 2, 1 htr in every dc. Turn.

Row 4 (WS): ch 1, sl st 1 in each st.

Break yarn and fasten off.

Work the next flounce in the same way only 8 (10) 10 (12) rows closer to dc rib.

FINISHING
Weave in remaining ends.
Pull a length of elastic through the waist by inserting it in and out between tr sts on 1st round, leaving gaps of 4–5 sts in between. Steam and press pants under a dry cloth.

Tip

Anton's nappy pants can be crocheted with a lanolin yarn suitable for the crochet weight of the pattern.

Freja's skirt

This one-piece skirt is full and slouchy. It has a double-crochet rib and an elastic waistband, so it fits snugly and can be adjusted to the perfect size. It is worked in half treble from the waist down. The length can be adjusted to fit an individual child.

Sizes
3 (6) 9 (12) 24 months

Measurements
Length: approx. 22 (25) 28 (31) 34cm
Waist: adjustable with elastic

Yarn
Filcolana Anina, 100% superwash merino, 210 metres/50g
Colour: brown 975 or blue 818
Quantity: 100 (150) 150 (200) 200g

Other materials
Elastic: approx. 50–60cm long and 1.5cm wide

Crochet hooks
2.5mm and 3mm

Tension
27 htr BLO x 19 rounds = 10 x 10cm

Note
Turning chains are not counted in the total number of stitches.
Close each round on 2nd and 3rd tier with 1 sl st in 1st htr through both loops.
A fan increase is a double increase. Simply work 3 htr stitches in the same stitch.

Pattern
All sts are worked BLO from row/round 2 unless otherwise stated in pattern.

RIB

Work 11 ch with 2.5mm hook.

Row 1: 1 dc in 2nd ch from hook, 1 dc in every subsequent ch (10 sts). Turn.

Row 2: ch 1, dc (BLO) in every st (10 sts). Turn.

Rep row 2 until a total of 110 (121) 126 (132) 140 rows of dc rib have been worked. Then work ribs together RS to RS to form a ring by working sts tog 2 by 2 through both layers with sl sts.
Do not break yarn.

SKIRT

Change to 3mm hook and work around the ring of dc rib as follows:

1st tier

Round 1 (RS): 3 ch, 110 (121) 126 (132) 140 tr around rib edge – 1 st in every row. Close round with 1 sl st in 1st tr through both loops.

Round 1 was worked in tr because there should be room to pull a length of elastic through at the waist on this round.
Place a sl st on RS.

Round 2 (again from RS): 2 ch, *1 htr (remember to work BLO) in next 9 sts, 1 fan inc (through both loops)*, rep from * to * around. Close round with 1 sl st in 1st htr

through both loops (132 (145) 152 (159) 168 sts). Turn and work the opposite way around.

Round 3 (WS): ch 2, 1 htr in every st in the round. Close round with 1 sl st in 1st htr through both loops (132 (145) 152 (159) 168 sts). Turn.

Round 4 (RS): ch 2, 1 htr in every st in the round. Close round with 1 sl st in 1st htr through both loops (132 (145) 152 (159) 168 sts). Turn.

Rep rounds 3 and 4 until first tier measures 6 (7) 8 (9) 10cm from rib edge. Finish with a round from RS without turning before 1st round on second tier.

Second tier

Round 1 (again from RS): 2 ch, *1 htr BLO for next 3 sts, 1 fan inc (through both loops)*, rep from * to * around (198 (218) 228 (239) 252 sts). Turn and work the opposite way around.

Round 2 (WS): 2 ch, 1 htr in every st around (198 (218) 228 (239) 252 sts). Turn.

Round 3 (RS): ch 2, 1 htr in every st around (198 (218) 228 (239) 252 sts). Turn. Rep rounds 2 and 3 until second tier measures 6 (7) 8 (9) 10cm.

Finish with a round from RS without turning before 1st round on third tier.

3rd tier

Round 1 (again from RS): 2 ch, *1 htr (still working BLO) in next 3 sts, 1 fan inc (through both loops)*, rep from * to * around (298 (327) 342 (359) 378 sts). Turn and work the opposite way around.

Round 2 (WS): 2 ch, 1 htr in every st around (298 (327) 342 (359) 378 sts). Turn.

Round 3 (RS): ch 2, 1 htr in every st around (298 (327) 342 (359) 378 sts). Turn.

Rep rounds 2 and 3 until third tier measures 7 (8) 9 (10) 11cm or desired length.

Finish the edge from RS, working 1 sl st in every st through both loops.
Break yarn and finish off.

FINISHING

Weave in the last ends.
Pull a length of elastic through the waist by inserting and pulling it out between tr on 1st round after rib, at 4–5 st intervals.
Steam and press the skirt under a dry cloth.

Tip

For summer, a linen, bamboo or cotton yarn is the obvious choice.

Tip

You can be inventive and crochet a picot edge or crab stitch edge instead of finishing with slip stitches (see p. 31).

William's vest

*William's vest is worked in one piece, in double crochet rib, from side to side.
The vest is easy to put on and take off as it can be opened all the way at the top with
buttons on each shoulder. To create a better fit, slip-stitch rib is crocheted into the
armhole and neckline.*

Sizes
3 (6) 9 (12) 24 months

Measurements
Length: approx. 22 (25) 30 (32) 35cm
Chest width: approx. 38 (42) 46 (48) 52cm

Yarn
Gepard CottonWool 3 Organic, 50% merino
and 50% cotton, 230 metres/50g
Colour: purple 807
Quantity: 100 (100) 100 (150) 150g

Other materials
4 (6) 6 (6) 6 pearl buttons: approx. 1.5cm in
diameter

Crochet hook
3mm

Tension
27–28 dc BLO x 34 rows = 10 x 10cm

Note
Make sure you work the very last st on a
row; it can be hard to find when working
BLO.

Turning chains are not counted in the total
stitch count.

Make sure that the loops are relatively loose
on the hook when working BLO, otherwise
it can be difficult to work.

Pattern
All sts are worked BLO from row 2 unless
otherwise stated in the pattern.

Buttonholes
Work 2 ch and skip 2 sts. On next row work
2 dc in 2 ch-sp.
Work buttonholes 4 sts from edge of
shoulder straps on back piece.

FRONT PIECE

Start on the right side of the vest.

Work 48 (53) 58 (63) 73 ch with 3mm hook. Make sure not to work ch too tight as this is the side seam.

Row 1 (WS): 1 dc in 2nd ch from hook, 1 dc in every subsequent ch (47 (52) 57 (62) 72 sts). Turn.

Row 2 (RS): ch 1, dc in every st BLO until 8 sts remain, sl st 1 in each of these 8 sts (47 (52) 57 (62) 72 sts). Turn.

Row 3 (WS): ch 1, 8 sl sts BLO, dc 1 BLO (47 (52) 57 (62) 72 sts). Reverse.

Rep rows 2 and 3 until there are a total of 6 (8) 8 (10) 10 rows. Finish with 2nd row and work 18 (24) 30 (30) 32 ch for right shoulder strap in continuation of last row. This is the side piece and armhole on the right side. Chain stitch rib is in the armhole.

Row 7 (9) 9 (11) 11 (WS): 1 dc in 2nd ch from hook and in all sts in row (64 (75) 86 (91) 103 sts).

Work back and forth with 64 (75) 86 (91) 103 dc until a total of 18 (22) 22 (24) 26 rows have been worked on shoulder strap. Turn without ch.

Row 25 (31) 31 (35) 37 (WS): 1 sl st in the first 13 (15) 17 (17) 19 sts through both loops, ch 1 (to get level), dc 1 in rem sts over row (total 64 (75) 86 (91) 103 sts). Turn. This is the 1st row of the neckline.

Row 26 (32) 32 (36) 38 (RS): ch 1, dc 1 in each st in row (51 (60) 69 (74) 84 sts). Turn.

Row 27 (33) 33 (37) 39 (WS): ch 1, sl st in each of first 8 sts, dc 1 in rem sts (51 (60) 69 (74) 84 sts). Turn.

Row 28 (34) 34 (38) 40 (RS): ch 1, dc 1 in each st until 8 sts remain, 1 sl st in last 8 sts (51 (60) 69 (74) 84 sts). Turn.

Rep last 2 rows until there are 14 (16) 18 (22) 24 rows in neckline.

Row 39 (47) 49 (57) 61 (WS): 1 ch, 1 dc in each st (51 (60) 69 (74) 84 sts). Turn.

Row 40 (48) 50 (58) 62 (RS): ch 1, dc 1 in 51 (60) 69 (74) 84 sts, work 14 (16) 18 (18) 20 ch for left shoulder strap. Turn.

Row 41 (49) 51 (59) 63 (WS): 1 dc in 2nd ch from hook and in all sts in row (total 64 (75) 86 (91) 103 sts). Turn.

Row 42 (50) 52 (60) 64 (RS): ch 1, dc 1 in all sts (total 64 (75) 86 (91) 103 sts). Turn.

Work rows back and forth with 64 (75) 86 (91) 103 dc until left shoulder strap has a total of 18 (22) 22 (24) 26 rows. Turn without ch.

Row 59 (71) 73 (83) 89 (WS): 1 sl st in the first 17 (23) 29 (29) 21 sl sts, ch 1, dc 1 in rem sts (total 47 (52) 57 (62) 72 sts) Turn.

Row 60 (72) 74 (84) 90 (RS): ch 1, dc 1 in each st until 8 sts rem, in which work 1 sl st (47 (52) 57 (62) 72 sts). Turn.

Row 61 (73) 75 (85) 91 (WS): ch 1, 8 sl sts, dc 1 in rem sts (47 (52) 57 (62) 72 sts). Turn.

Rep these last 2 rows until there are a total of 6 (8) 8 (10) 10 rows on side piece/armhole on left side.
A total of 64 (78) 80 (92) 98 rows have been worked on front piece.
Do not break yarn.

BACK

Rows 1–6 (8) 8 (10) 10 (WS): continue back and forth with the same stitch distribution as described in side piece/armhole of front piece. Work 26 (32) 38 (38) 40 ch for shoulder strap in extension of last row. Turn.

Row 7 (9) 9 (11) 11 (WS): 1 dc in 2nd ch from hook, 1 dc in every st of round (72 (83) 94 (99) 111 sts). Turn.

Row 8 (10) 10 (12) 12 (RS): ch 1, dc 1 in each st (72 (83) 94 (99) 111 sts). Turn.

Work dc back and forth until a total of 18 (22) 22 (24) 26 rows have been worked on shoulder strap. Remember to work 2 (3) 3 (3) 3 buttonholes on the left shoulder strap of the back, on row 5 and 14 of shoulder strap (row 4, 11 and 19) row 4, 11 and 19 (row 4, 12 and 20) row 4, 13 and 22. Turn without ch.

Row 25 (31) 31 (35) 37: 1 sl st in the first 12 (12) 12 (12) 13 ch through both loops, ch 1 (to come level with dc), dc 1 in each st in row (total 60 (71) 82 (87) 98 sts). Turn.

Row 26 (32) 32 (36) 38: ch 1, dc 1 in each dc row (do not work the last 12 (12) 12 (12) 13 sts) (total 60 (71) 82 (87) 98 sts). Turn.

Row 27 (33) 33 (37) 39: ch 1, sl st in first 8 sts, 1 dc in rem sts in round (60 (71) 82 (87) 98 sts). Turn.

Row 28 (34) 34 (38) 40: ch 1, dc 1 in each st, until 8 sts rem, then work in sl sts (60 (71) 82 (87) 98 sts). Turn. Rep the last 2 rows until there are a total of 14 (16) 18 (22) 24 rows for neckline.

Row 39 (47) 49 (57) 61 (WS): ch 1, dc 1 in each st in round (60 (71) 82 (87) 98 sts). Turn.

Row 40 (48) 50 (58) 62 (RS): ch 1, dc 1 in each st. Work 13 (13) 13 (13) 14 ch for shoulder strap. Turn.

Row 41 (49) 51 (59) 63 (WS): 1 dc in 2nd ch from hook and in every st (72 (83) 94 (99) 111 sts). Turn. Work right shoulder strap in the same way as left shoulder strap of back. Remember buttonholes. When 18 (22) 22 (24) 26 rows have been worked, turn without ch.

Row 59 (71) 73 (83) 89 (WS): 25 (31) 37 (37) 39 sl st through both loops, ch 1 (to come level with dc), dc 1 (again BLO) to end (47 (52) 57 (62) 72 sts). Turn.

Row 60 (72) 74 (84) 90 (RS): Ch 1, dc 1 in each st, for last 8 sts in which ch is worked (BLO, as it is a side piece/armhole) (47 (52) 57 (62) 72 sts). Turn.

Row 61 (73) 75 (85) 91 (WS): 1 ch, 1 sl st in the first 8 sts, 1 dc in last sts (47 (52) 57 (62) 72 sts). Turn.

Rep the last 2 rows until a total of 6 rows have been worked, (8) 8 (10) 10 rows in armhole and a total of 64 (78) 80 (92) 98 rows have been worked on back.

Place vest double on right side, RS to RS; work sts tog 2 by 2 with sl sts through both layers.
Break yarn and fasten off.

FINISHING

Sew on buttons and weave in last ends. Gently steam and press vest under a dry cloth.

This mustard yellow vest is crocheted in Krea Deluxe Organic Wool 1, colour 09.

Karl Viggo's trousers

This design can be crocheted either as shorts or as long trousers. The pattern is worked in half treble crochet with double crochet rib at the waist. You can adjust the length as desired. Choose your own colour for the trousers, as the pattern lists several options for yarns, all of which have a wide colour range. The shorts shown here are crocheted in Gepard Cotton Wool 3, 534 navy blue, while the long trousers are worked in Önling No 12, colour 1 light grey. The elasticated waistband can be adjusted to fit the baby perfectly.

Sizes
3 (6) 9 (12) 24 months

Measurements
Waist: approx. 40 (42) 44 (44) 46cm
Hip width: approx. 48 (52) 56 (57) 59cm
Leg length of shorts: approx. 8 (9) 9 (10) 11cm
Leg length of long trousers: approx. 19 (22) 26 (28) 30cm

Yarn
Önling No 12, 55% wool and 45% cotton, 800 metres/115g
Quantity: 1 ball for shorts and long trousers – all sizes
or
Gepard CottonWool 3 Organic, 50% wool and 50% cotton, 230 metres/50g
Quantity: 100 (100) 150 (150) 200g for shorts. For long trousers use 50g more
or
Gepard My Fine Wool, 100% superfine merino, 233 metres/50g
Quantity: 100 (100) 150 (150) 200g for shorts. For long trousers use 50g more

Other materials
Elastic: approx. 60–70cm and 1.5cm wide for the waist and approx. 40cm for the two trouser legs

Crochet hooks
2.5mm and 3mm

Tension
28 htr BLO x 18 rows = 10 x 10cm

Note
Turning chains are not counted in the total number of stitches.
Close each round with 1 sl st in 1st htr through both loops. Join on round is on baby's right side. Place a stitch marker on RS of front piece and between fan increases, preferably as a thread in contrasting colour to follow the gusset up round by round. Piece is then divided to continue working on each trouser leg.

Pattern
All sts are worked BLO from row 2 unless otherwise stated in pattern.

RIB

Work 11 ch with 2.5mm hook.

Row 1: 1 dc in 2nd ch from hook, 1 dc in every subsequent ch (10 sts). Turn.

Row 2: ch 1, dc in every st of BLO (10 sts). Turn.

Rep row 2 until a total of 110 (121) 132 (132) 140 rows of dc rib have been worked. Then work ribs together RS to RS to form a ring by working sts tog 2 by 2 through both layers with sl sts.
Do not break yarn.

PANTS

Change to 3mm hook.

Round 1 (RS): 3 ch, 110 (121) 132 (132) 140 tr around dc rib; 1 st per row. Close round with 1 sl st in 1st tr through both loops (total 110 (121) 132 (132) 140 sts). Turn and work the opposite way around.

Round 1 was worked in tr because there should be room to pull the elastic through at the waist on this round.

Round 2 (WS): 2 ch, 1 htr (remember to work BLO from here) in every st in the round, at the same time work 22 (25) 26 (28) 28 incs evenly spaced (inc in approx every 5th st). Close round with 1 sl st in 1st htr (132 (146) 158 (160) 168 sts). Turn.

Round 3 (RS): ch 2, 1 htr in the first 66 (73) 79 (80) 84 sts (front piece), PM and let it follow the side of the piece, 1 htr in rem 66 (73) 79 (80) 84 sts (back piece). Close round with 1 sl st in 1st htr (132 (146) 158 (160) 168 sts). Turn.

Round 4 (WS): ch 2, 1 htr in first 66 (73) 79 (80) 84 sts (back piece), PM, 1 htr in

remaining 66 (73) 79 (80) 84 sts (front piece). Close round with 1 sl st in 1st htr (132 (146) 158 (160) 168 sts). Turn.

Rep rounds 3 and 4 until 18 (22) 24 (26) 28 rounds have been worked in total from dc rib. Piece measures approx. 14 (16) 17 (18) 19cm. Work last round with htr from WS.

WEDGES FRONT AND BACK

Continue in htr rib.
NB: remember that fan increase is worked through both loops and only from RS.

Round 19 (23) 25 (27) 29 round (RS): 2 ch, 1 htr in first 32 (35) 38 (39) 41 sts, 1 fan inc (see p. 19), PM, 0 (1) 1 (0) 0 htr, 1 fan inc, 64 (70) 76 (78) 82 htr, 1 fan inc, PM, 0 (1) 1 (0) 0 htr, 1 fan inc, 1 htr in the next 32 (35) 38 (39) 41 htr. Close with 1 sl st in 1st htr (total 140 (154) 166 (168) 176 sts). Turn.

Insert a PM in the middle of the 3 sts in each of the 4 fan shapes, and also let these sl sts follow the piece up from round to round.

Note: Fan increases should be worked on top of each other on top of the middle of the 3 sts. Make sure to work the inc sts between fans in rib pattern from round to round. Increase by 2 sts in the wedge itself for every round inc. Also increase the number of stitches in the trousers by 4 sts for each RS round worked fanwise.

Round 20 (24) 26 (28) 30 (WS): ch 2, 1 htr in every st (total 140 (154) 166 (168) 176 sts). Turn.

Round 21 (25) 27 (29) 31 (RS): ch 2, 33 (36) 39 (40) 42 htr, 1 fan inc, 2 (3) 3 (2) 2 htr, slip marker, 1 fan inc, 66 (72) 78 (80) 84 htr, 1 fan inc, 2 (3) 3 (2) 2 htr, slip marker, 33 (36) 39 (40) 42 htr (148 (162) 174 (176) 184 sts). Turn.

Round 22 (26) 28 (30) 32: ch 2, htr 1 in every st on round (148 (162) 174 (176) 184 sts). Turn.

Rep these 2 rounds until there are a total of 4 (5) 5 (6) 6 inc rounds from RS to wedge. Finish with a round of htr without inc, from WS. There are 164 (186) 198 (208) 216 sts in total.

Break yarn and finish off.

BOTTOM

Work a bottom piece in htr rib over 8 (11) 11 (12) 14 sts on front piece wedge as follows:

Row 1 (RS): join yarn in first st inside fan, ch 2, 1 htr in each of the 8 (11) 11 (12) 14 sts in wedge. Turn.

Row 2 (WS): ch 2, 1 htr in every st (8 (11) 11 (12) 14 sts). Turn.

Rep row 2 until there are a total of 5 (6) 6 (6) 7 rows on bottom piece.

Now place the bottom piece RS over the 8 (11) 11 (12) 14 sts on back piece. NB: Make sure you count the sts so that there are the same number of sts on both legs, i.e. 74 (82) 88 (92) 94 sts. Then work sts tog with sl sts, 2 and 2 and through both layers.
Break the yarn and fasten off.

SHORT TROUSER LEGS

Work htr rib along side of bottom piece and in 74 (82) 88 (92) 94 sts on each trouser leg as follows.

Round 1: Attach yarn from RS on inside of right trouser leg, ch 2. Along one side of bottom piece work htr sts starting from 2nd (3rd) 3rd (3rd) 3rd row of front piece.

The join on the trouser leg should be here, on the front of both right and left trouser legs. Work 3 htr for every 2 rows (total 7 (9) 9 (9) 10 sts).

Work htr in each of the next 74 (82) 88 (92) 94 sts, then the last htr on bottom piece. Close round with 1 sl st in 1st htr through both loops (total 81 (91) 97 (101) 104 sts). Turn.

Round 2 (WS): ch 2, htr 1, dec 1, htr 1 in every st in the round (80 (90) 96 (100) 103 sts). Turn.

Rep round 2 from RS and WS a total of 7 (10) 10 (11) 12 times. A total of 74 (81) 87 (90) 102 sts remain on piece.

Work straight without decs until there are a total of 14 (15) 16 (18) 20 rounds on trouser leg or to desired length. The leg measures approx. 8 (9) 9 (10) 11cm from bottom piece.

Finish the edge with 1 sl st in every st from RS of piece.
Break yarn and fasten off.

Work the other leg in the same way, but this time start just opposite, on the other side of the bottom piece.

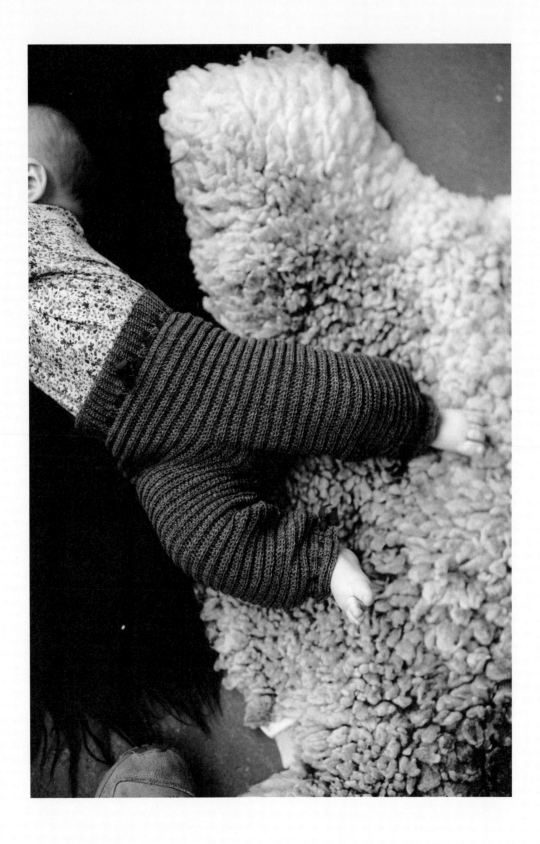

LONG TROUSER LEGS

Work long trouser legs following the description for the legs of the shorts until 8 (11) 11 (12) 13 rounds have been worked.

Continue with 1 dec every 4th round a further 5 (5) 6 (6) 9 times. 69 (76) 81 (84) 93 sts remain.

Work straight until trouser leg measures 19 (22) 26 (28) 30cm from bottom piece or to desired length.

Finish the edge from RS, working 1 sl st in every st through both loops.
Break yarn and fasten off.

FINISHING

Weave in any remaining ends.
Pull a length of elastic through waist by passing it in and out between tr on 1st round, at 4–5 st intervals.
Tie a knot on the elastic at the centre front of the trousers.
In the same way, pull a length of elastic in 3rd round from bottom edge of long trouser legs.
Gently steam and press the trousers under a dry cloth.

Tip

Feel free to use other yarn types with the same crochet weight as indicated in this pattern. The trousers will work in wool, bamboo, linen, cotton, alpaca and silk and blends of these fibres; for example, Sandnes Sunday sock yarn, such as Filcolana Anina, which has a running length of 210 metres, is a good alternative.

Jens' & Julie's tops

This patterned top features a round yoke of half treble rib. It is worked top down in one piece. There is a slit at the back that is closed with a single button at the neck. The top is therefore easy to put on over a baby's head. The body and sleeves have a two-colour crochet pattern. Julie's top is finished with a peplum ruffle. Jens' top is finished with an elastic band.

Size
3 (6) 12 (24) months

Measurements
Length: approx. 25 (30) 33 (36)cm
Chest width: approx. 45 (52) 56 (60)cm
Sleeve length: approx. 17 (20) 22 (25)cm
Sleeve width: approx. 14 (18) 20 (21)cm

Yarn
Julie's top
Krea Deluxe Organic Wool 1, 100% organic wool, 145 metres/50g
Colour A: off-white 01
Colour B: light yellow 04
Quantity: 150 (150) 200 (200)g colour A, 100 (100) 150 (150)g colour B

Jens' top
Sandnes Babyull Lanett, 100% merino wool, 175 metres/50g
and
Rowan Finest, 50% wool, 20% cashmere, 30% alpaca, 87 metres/25g
Colour A: Rowan Finest, grey-green SH068
Colour B: Babyull Lanett, black 1099
Quantity: 100 (125) 125 (150)g colour A, 50 (100) 100 (100)g colour B

Other materials
1 button: 1.5–2cm in diameter
Elastic: approx. 50–60cm long

Crochet hook
3.5mm

Tension
23 htr BLO x 18 rows = 10 x 10cm
23 dc x 27 rows in pattern = 10 x 10cm

Note
Make sure that you work the very last st on a row; it can be hard to find when working BLO.
Turning chains are not counted in the total number of stitches.

Place a stitch marker on the RS of the piece.

Work rows of htr rib on yoke. Work the first 5 and last 5 sts as dc rib, tightening the slit at the back.
Make sure incs are evenly spaced on yoke and not just above each other from row to row to keep the edge nicely rounded.

On the body there is a gathering on the back row on the right side.

See below for how to work the two-colour pattern.

When changing colour, pull the new colour yarn through sts at beg of round. Only then work the next stitch (as shown in pattern) with the new colour yarn. Make sure that the yarn not in use is brought up to the WS of the piece.

Two-colour pattern: divisible by 4 sts
Round 1 (RS): change to colour B, ch 1, dc 1 in next 3 sts, *ch 2, skip 1 st, dc 1 in next 3 sts*, rep from * to * around. Finish round with 2 ch, skip 1 st, 1 sl st in 1st dc. Turn piece and work the opposite way.

Round 2: ch 1, dc in 1st st, *ch 2, skip 2-ch space, dc in next 3 sts*, rep from * to * around. Finish round with 2 ch, skip ch-space and work 1 dc in each of the last 2 sts. Close round with 1 sl st in 1st dc. Turn.

Round 3 (RS): change to colour A, ch 1, * 1 dc, ch 2, skip 1 st, ch 1 in next st, then work 1 spike stitch as follows: 1 tr in the round around 2-ch space and straight down in st 3 rounds below*, rep from * to * around. Finish with 1 sl st in 1st dc. Turn.

Round 4: Ch 1, 3 dc, *ch 2, skip 2-ch space, dc 1 in next 3 sts*, rep from * to * around. Finish with ch 2, skip 2-ch space, and close round with 1 sl st in 1st dc. Turn.

Round 5 (RS): change to colour B, ch 1, *1 dc in next st, then work 1 spike stitch as follows: 1 tr around 2-ch space and straight down in st on 2nd round; 1 dc, 2 ch, skip 1 st*, rep from * to * around. Finish round with 1 sl st in 1st dc. Turn.

Round 6: Ch 1, dc 1 in 1st st, *ch 2, skip 2-ch space, dc 1 in next 3 sts*, rep from * to * around. Finish with 2 ch and skip 2-ch space, 1 dc in last 2 sts, and close round with 1 sl st in 1st dc. Turn.

Rep rounds 3–6 of pattern to measurements given in pattern below or to desired length.

Finish pattern with the following 2 rounds:
Round 7 (RS): change to color A, *1 dc in first 3 sts, 1 spike stitch as follows: 1 tr around 2-ch space and straight down in st 3 rounds below*, rep * to * around, ending with 1 dc in last 3 sts.

Round 8 (again from RS): 1 dc in every st round.

YOKE

Measure 2 metres of yarn in colour A before working the first ch. Leave this hanging at the beginning to work sl sts in neckline. Work the sl st as soon as you can to avoid the yarn hanging during the rest of the work. This is done as follows:

With the long end from the cast-on, work 1 sl st in every st from RS. Crochet 5 ch for button loop, and fasten loop with a few sl sts a little further down the slit.

Work 62 (68) 76 (80) ch with colour A.

Row 1 (RS): 1 htr in 3rd ch from hook, 1 htr in every subsequent ch (60 (66) 74 (78) sts). Turn.

Row 2: ch 1, dc 1 (remember to work BLO from now on) in first 5 sts, htr 1 and at the same time 8 incs evenly spaced in next 50 (56) 64 (68) sts, dc 1 in last 5 sts (68 (74) 82 (86) sts). Turn.

NB: make sure that the increases are not aligned from row to row to keep the edges of the piece rounded rather than jagged.

Row 3: ch 1, dc 1 in the first 5 sts, htr 1 and at the same time 8 incs evenly spaced in the next 58 (64) 72 (76) sts, dc 1 in the last 5 sts (76 (82) 90 (94) sts). Turn.

Row 4: ch 1, dc 1 in the first 5 sts, htr 1 and at the same time 8 incs evenly spaced in the next 66 (72) 80 (84) sts, dc 1 in the last 5 sts (84 (90) 98 (102) sts) Turn.

Rep increases until a total of 10 (12) 14 (14) rows have been worked with increases. When yoke is finished, there will be a total of 11 (13) 15 (15) rows and 140 (162) 186 (190) sts on row.
Break yarn and fasten off.
Now work on sleeves, front piece and back piece separately.

BODY

Work in the round in two-colour pattern on body sts.
Divide the piece by counting from RS 20 (23) 26 (27) sts (back piece), 30 (35) 41 (41) sts (sleeve stitches to be worked later), 40 (46) 52 (54) sts (front piece), 30 (35) 41 (41) sts (sleeve) and 20 (23) 26 (27) sts (back piece).

Continue working with colour A and dc and no longer work BLO.

Round 1 (RS): Attach yarn to piece and work 1 ch, 1 dc in last 20 (23) 26 (27) sts of yoke (back piece). Then work dc directly across the opening at the back to close the slit: dc in the first 20 (23) 26 (27) sts of yoke (back piece). Work 6 (8) 9 (9) ch in armhole, skip 30 (35) 41 (41) sts (sleeve), 1 dc in each of the next 40 (46) 52 (54) sts (front piece), ch 6 (8) 9 (9) in armhole, skip last 30 (35) 41 (41) sts over (sleeve), close round with 1 sl st in 1st dc (92 (108) 122 (126) sts).

Round 2 (again from RS): 1 ch, beg round 1 of two-colour pattern. Follow pattern in all body sts while working 6 (8) 2 (6) incs evenly spaced – avoid making incs in the 6 (8) 9 (9) ch under armholes (total 98 (116) 124 (132) sts). Turn.

Tip

You can crochet the top in many different yarn types. Double thread alpaca, which runs at 400 metres/50g, is soft and gives the top a certain weight. Alternatively, crochet the top in bamboo, Tencel, linen or cotton for summer use. Just observe the crochet tension indicated when choosing an alternative yarn.

Follow the colour pattern back and forth on round and work straight until Julie's top measures approx. 19 (23) 26 (29)cm and Jens' top measures 23 (28) 30 (33)cm or desired length. Finish the colour pattern with rounds 7–8.

Continue to the hem on Jens' top or the peplum on Julie's top.

HEM
On Jens' top work 10 rounds in a row with dc – all rounds from RS. On round 4 work 2 holes in left side as follows: *1 ch, skip 1 st*, 3 dc, rep from * to * one more time. On next round work 1 dc in ch-space.

PEPLUM
On next round from RS work peplum in htr rib with colour A.

Round 1 (RS): 2 ch, 1 tr (htr in through both loops) in every st in the round, close round with 1 sl st in 1st htr through both loops to inc each stitch (196 (232) 248 (264) sts). Turn piece and work the opposite way.

Round 2 (WS): 2 ch, 1 htr BLO in every st, close round with 1 sl st in 1st htr through both loops (196 (232) 248 (264) sts.

Rep round 2 from RS and WS until flounce measures 6 (6) 7 (7)cm. Finish 1 sl st in every st from RS through both loops.
Break yarn and finish off.

SLEEVE
The sleeve is worked in the round in the two-colour pattern. Start with colour A in the middle of the ch of the armhole.
Work through both loops.
Round 1 (RS): Attach yarn to piece and work 1 ch, 1 dc in each of the 30 (35) 41 (41) sts in sleeve and the 6 (8) 9 (9) ch in armhole. Close round with 1 sl st in 1st dc (36 (43) 50 (50) sts). Turn.

Round 2 (WS): ch 1, dc 1 in each st in the round, at the same time adjust the number of stitches to 36 (44) 48 (52) sts, as stitch count must be divisible by 4 to fit pattern. Close round with 1 sl st in 1st st (36 (44) 48 (52) sts). Turn.

Round 3 (RS): Begin two-colour pattern – round 1.

Continue working and following pattern until sleeve measures 16 (19) 21 (24)cm from armhole or desired length. Finish the pattern with rounds 7–8.

Finish sleeve from RS with dc, working 7 (8) 9 (10) decs evenly; 29 (36) 39 (42) sts remain.

Work another round with dc and finally finish the edge with 1 sl st in every st from RS – not too tight.
Break yarn and fasten off.
Work the other sleeve in the same way.

FINISHING
Weave in the last ends and sew a button at the neck. On Jens' top, fold edge over to inside and sew in place. Pass a length of elastic through the loop and out through the holes in the left side of the top. Tie a knot in the elastic. Gently steam and press the top under a dry cloth.

Antony's tunic

Antony's tunic can be buttoned up all the way on both sides, making it easy to take on and off. It is worked in one piece with two strands of Isager Alpaca 1. There are increases in a round yoke of half treble crochet rib and a button in the middle back of the neck. The front and back pieces are worked separately from the yoke.

Sizes
3 (6) 12 (24) months

Measurements
Length: approx. 30 (34) 38 (44)cm
Chest width: approx. 46 (48) 50 (52)cm

Yarn
Isager Alpaca 1, 100% alpaca, 400 metres/50g
Colour A: grey eco 4S
Colour B: dusty pink 61
Quantity: 100 (100) 150 (150)g colour A, 100 (100) 100 (100)g colour B

Other materials
7 (7) 9 (9) mother-of-pearl buttons: approx. 1.5cm in diameter

Crochet hook
3.5mm

Tension
Worked with two strands Alpaca 1
26 htr BLO x 18 rows = 10 x 10cm

Note
Make sure you work the very last st on a row; it can be hard to find when working BLO.
Turning chains are not counted in the total stitch count.
Feel free to put a stitch marker on RS.
Make sure increases are evenly spaced on the yoke and not right on top of each other from row to row so the piece is rounded and not jagged on the edges.
There are panels of dc rib on each side of the lower parts of the garment.

See p. 19 for how to work spike stitches.

Pattern
All sts on yoke are worked BLO from row 2 unless otherwise stated in pattern. The two-colour pattern is worked in dc through both loops and no longer BLO.

When changing colour, pull the new colour yarn through at last pull-through on last st in old colour. Make sure that the yarn not in use is brought up to the WS of the piece.

Two-colour pattern: divisible by 4 + 3 sts

Row 1 (RS): change to colour B. 1 dc in first 3 sts, *2 ch, skip 1 st, 1 dc in next 3 sts*, rep from * to * to end.

Row 2: 1 dc in first 3 sts, *2 ch, skip ch-space, 1 dc in next 3 sts*, rep from * to * to end.

Row 3 (RS): change to colour A. *1 dc, 2 ch, skip 1 st, 1 dc in next st, then work 1 spike stitch as follows: 1 tr around 2-ch space and straight down in st 3 rows below*, rep from * to * to end. Finish with 1 dc, 2 ch, skip 1 st, 1 dc.

Row 4: 1 dc, *2 ch, skip ch-space, 1 dc in next 3 sts*, rep from * to * to end. Finish with 2 ch, skip ch-space, 1 dc.

Row 5: Change to colour B. *1 dc in next st, then work 1 spike stitch as follows: 1 tr around 2-ch space and straight down in st on 2nd row; 1 dc, 2 ch, skip 1 st*, rep from * to * to end. Omit the 2 ch on the last repeat.

Row 6: 1 dc in first 3 sts *2 ch, skip ch-space, 1 dc in next 3 sts*, rep from * to *.

Rep rows 3–6 to measurements given below or to desired length.
Finish pattern with the following 2 rows:
Row 7: Change to colour A. *1 dc in first 3 sts, then 1 spike stitch as follows: 1 tr around 2-ch space and straight down in st 3 rows below*, rep from * to * to end, and finish with 1 dc in the last 3 sts.

Row 8: Work 1 dc in every st in row.

Buttonholes
From RS: 2 dc, 2 ch, skip 2 sts, 4 dc, work pattern over 79 (91) 103 (111) sts, 4 dc, ch 2, skip 2 sts, 2 dc. On next row work 2 dc in ch-spaces.
Work buttonholes on every 16th row 3 (3) 4 (4) times in total.

YOKE

Work a yoke with htr rib.

Leave approx. 2 metres of yarn in colour A hanging at beg, which you will use to work sl st edge etc. for neckline. Work sl st as soon as you can to avoid the yarn hanging for the duration of the work. This is done as follows: With the long end from the cast-on, work 1 sl st in every st from RS. Crochet 5 ch for button loop, and fasten loop with a few sl sts a little further down the slit.

Work 62 (68) 76 (86) ch with two strands Isager Alpaca 1.

Row 1: (RS) 1 htr in 3rd ch from hook and then 1 htr in every ch over (60 (66) 74 (84) sts in total). Turn.

Row 2 (WS): ch 1, dc 1 (BLO) in first 5 sts, htr 1 BLO while working 8 incs evenly over next 50 (56) 64 (74) sts, dc 1 in last 5 sts (68 (74) 82 (92) sts). Turn.

Row 3 (RS): ch 1, dc 1 in first 5 sts, htr 1, at the same time 8 incs evenly spaced in next 58 (64) 72 (82) sts, dc 1 in last 5 sts (76 (82) 90 (100) sts). Turn.

Row 4 (WS): ch 1, dc 1 in first 5 sts, htr 1 and work 8 incs evenly spaced in next 66 (72) 80 (90) sts, dc 1 in last 5 sts (84 (90) 98 (108) sts). Turn.

Make sure that the increases are not made on top of each other from row to row so the piece is smooth and rounded and not jagged on the edge.
Inc by 2 sts between rows from row to row. At the beg and end of a row inc 1 st before and after working an increase.

Rep row with increases 10 (12) 14 (14) times on yoke until in total there are 11 (13) 15 (15) rows and 140 (162) 186 (196) sts on row. Break yarn and cast off.

BOTTOM PART OF TUNIC

Now work on front and back pieces, dividing piece by counting from RS, 20 (23) 26 (28) sts (back piece), 30 (35) 41 (42) sts (shoulder sts not worked), 40 (46) 52 (56) sts (front piece), 30 (35) 41 (42) sts (shoulder) and 20 (23) 26 (28) sts (back piece). Feel free to insert a stitch marker between the pieces.

BACK

Work in colour A starting with the last 20 (23) 26 (28) sts of yoke. Work rib edges on each side in colour A.

Row 1 (RS): join yarn, ch 1, dc 1 (no longer BLO) in each of last 20 (23) 26 (28) sts and directly over the first 20 (23) 26 (28) sts on yoke – slits are now closed at the back (40 (46) 52 (56) sts). Turn.

Row 2 (WS): 8 (9) 10 (11) ch, 1 dc in the 2nd ch from hook and in next 6 (7) 8 (9) dc in ch (this is dc rib at side), 1 tr in next 39 (45) 51 (55) sts, 1 dc in last st (79 (91) 103 (111) sts total – number of stitches to fit colour pattern) (total 86 (99) 112 (121) sts with dc rib on one side). Turn.

NB: on row 3, make sure you have two strands in colour A ready for dc rib on RS. This extra ball is worked on rows where pattern in the middle is worked with colour B.

Row 3: 8 (9) 10 (11) ch, 1 dc in 2nd ch from hook and in next 6 (7) 8 (9) sts (dc rib on other side). Change to colour B after the last of the 6 (7) 8 (9) dc, then follow 1st row of colour pattern (through both loops) over the middle 79 (91) 103 (111) sts, change to colour A, 7 (8) 9 (10) dc in BLO. There are 93 (107) 121 (131) sts in total with dc rib on both sides. Turn.

Row 4: Colour A, ch 1, 7 (8) 9 (10) dc BLO, follow 2nd row of colour pattern over the next 79 (91) 103 (111) sts, work the last 7 (8)

9 (10) dc BLO with colour A (93 (107) 121 (131) sts). Turn.

Continue working panels in dc rib and pattern as described until piece measures approx. 27 (31) 34 (40)cm. Finish pattern with row 7–8.

HEM EDGE

Work a final edge with colour A. The edge is a continuation of the dc rib as seen on the sides.

Row 1 (RS): ch 1, 7 (8) 9 (10) dc BLO, dc 1 through both loops in every st of the middle sts. Finish with 7 (8) 9 (10) dc BLO (93 (107) 121 (131) sts). Turn.

Row 2 (WS): ch 1, dc in all sts in row (93 (107) 121 (131) sts). Turn.

Rep row 2 10 more times alternately from RS and WS, for a total of 12 rows in edge.

Finish with 1 sl st in every st through both loops. Break yarn and fasten ends.

FRONT PIECE
Work with colour A and from RS 1 sl st in each of the next 7 (8) 9 (10) dc on dc rib of front piece and in 30 (35) 41 (42) sts of shoulder.
Continue with 1st row.

Row 1 (RS): ch 1 (to level with dc), dc 1 in next 40 (46) 52 (56) sts on yoke (40 (46) 52 (56) sts). Turn.
Row 2: as on back piece.
Row 3: as on back piece, but work buttonholes in the side dc rib.

Continue working on front piece as described on back piece. Remember buttonholes.

FINISHING
Weave in all remaining ends.
Sew buttons to both sides of back panel in dc rib, as well as one button at neck.
Work a sl st edge from RS with colour A similar to the edge in shoulder stitches and dc rib/sleeve yoke on the other side of tunic.
Gently steam and press the tunic under a dry cloth.

Tip

You can work a flounce around the yoke, as on Filippa's dress, p. 50.

Lucia's top

This top features a ruffle on a yoke with raglan sleeves. It is open all the way down and has buttons at the back yoke. The pattern includes half treble and treble rib. The yarn is light and fluffy with a long running length. It is relatively inelastic but comes in some beautiful colours. The yarn is not suitable for very small children because of the loose yarn fibres. Therefore, only sizes for 12 and 24 months are included. It is not easy to unravel the hairy yarn, so pay extra attention to the stitch count.

Size
12 (24) months

Measurements
Ample freedom of movement/chest width:
approx. 54 (60)cm
Body width: 74 (88)cm
Length: approx. 32 (37)cm

Yarn
Drops Brushed Alpaca Silk, 23% silk,
77% alpaca, 140 metres/25g
Colour: pink
Quantity: 100 (125)g

Other materials
3–4 pearl buttons: 1.5–2cm in diameter

Crochet hook
4mm

Tension
20 htr BLO x 15 rows = 10 x 10cm
20 tr BLO x 11 rows = 10 x 10cm

Note
Make sure you work the very last st on a row; it can be hard to find when working BLO with a bulky yarn.
Turning stitches are not counted in total stitch count.
Mark raglan increases with stitch markers as explained in pattern.
Let the stitch markers (preferably yarn in a contrasting colour) be carried forward for each row.
The first inc of the two worked around the stitch marker is worked in st just above the stitch marker.

Pattern
Work all sts BLO from row 2 unless otherwise stated in pattern.

Buttonholes
Work htr until 4 sts remain on row, then ch 1, skip 1 st and work 1 htr in last 3 sts. On next row work 1 htr in ch-space.
Rep buttonhole on every 4th row on yoke.

Tip

To compensate for the inelastic yarn, a transparent jewellery elastic can be inserted through a row under the yoke. The vest is very wide and open without elastic. With elastic, the width can be adjusted so that the vest fits each child as desired.

YOKE

Leave about 2 metres of yarn hanging at the beginning, which you will need to work the neckline with a slip stitch edge. Work the slip stitch edge as soon as you can, then you can avoid having the yarn hanging during the rest of the work. Work 1 sl st in every st from RS with the long end from cast-on.

Work 67 (83) ch.

Row 1 (RS): 1 htr in 3rd ch from hook, 1 htr in every subsequent ch (65 (81) sts). Turn.

Row 2 (WS): NOTE: work a buttonhole at the end of this row, inside the 14 (16) sts on the right back piece. Ch 2, 1 htr (remember to work BLO from now on) in 11 (13) sts (left back piece), PM, 10 (14) htr (shoulder sleeve), PM, 20 (24) htr (front piece), PM, 10 (14) htr, PM, 14 (16) htr (right back piece) (65 (81) sts). Turn.

Increases are made on each side of each of the 4 stitch markers.

Row 3: 2 ch, 1 htr in the first 13 (15) sts, inc 1, PM, inc 1, 8 (12) htr, inc 1, PM, inc 1, 18 (22) htr, 1 htr, PM, inc 1, 8 (12) htr, PM, inc 1, 10 (12) htr (73 (89) sts. Turn.

Row 4 (WS): ch 2, 11 (13) htr, inc 1, slip marker, inc 1, 10 (14) htr, inc 1, slip marker, inc 1, 20 (24) htr, inc 1, slip marker, inc 1, 10 (14) htr, inc 1, slip marker, inc 1, 14 (16) htr (81 (97) sts). Turn.

Rep rows 3 and 4 until 12 (14) rows with increases have been worked on yoke, inc 2 sts between stitch markers for each row. At the beginning and end of a row inc 1 st before and after a htr respectively. Remember buttonholes on every 4th row. A total of 14 (16) rows have been worked and there are 161 (193) sts on row.

BODY

Slip marker on yoke – divide into 23 (27) sts (back), 34 (42) sts (sleeve), 44 (52) sts (front piece), 34 (42) sts (sleeve), 26 (30) sts (back piece).

Cont BLO over front and back.

Row 1 (RS): ch 2, 1 htr in first 26 (30) sts, ch 5 (6) (armhole), skip 34 (42) sts, ch 1 in next 44 (52) sts, ch 5 (6) (armhole), skip 34 (42) sts, ch 1 in last 23 (27) sts (103 (121) sts total). Turn.

Row 2: ch 2, 6 htr, *1 tr, inc 1*, rep from * to * to last 6 sts (do not work increases in armhole chain) until last 6 htr (148 (176) sts). Turn.

Row 3: Ch 2, 6 htr, 130 (158) tr, 6 htr (148 (176) sts). Turn.

Row 4: ch 2, 6 htr, 130 (158) tr, 6 htr (148 (176) sts). Turn.

Rep rows 3 and 4 until piece measures 28 (33)cm or desired length.

Work 7 rows htr rib as bottom edge of garment. Finish with a row of 1 sl st in every st through both loops. Break yarn and finish off.

Tip

You can turn the top around so that the buttons are in the front. This will transform the piece into a short-sleeve cardigan. In this case, work the buttonholes further down the body.

SHORT SLEEVES

Work sleeves with tr BLO on every round. Remember to fit rib pattern so that you work BLO from the RS.

Round 1 (RS): Insert yarn in the middle of armholes, work 2 ch, 1 tr in same st, then 1 tr in each of the next ch, work 1 tr around the htr on last row on yoke, rather than into it (in this case the htr is in the horizontal position), 1 tr in each of the 34 (42) sts of sleeve, work again 1 tr around the htr on last row on yoke, and finish with 1 tr in each of the last ch in armholes. Close round with 1 sl st in 1st htr through both loops (44 (54 sts). Turn and work the other way around.

Round 2 (WS): ch 2, dec 1, in 1, dc 1 in each st in the round. Also work 1 dec in each side of sleeve where you worked around (rather than into) the htr in round 1. Close round with 1 sl st in 1st htr (41 (51) sts). Turn.

Round 3: ch 2, dc 1, dec 1, dc 1 in each st in the round. Close round with 1 sl st in 1st htr (40 (50) sts). Turn.

Rep round 3 until a total of 6 (8) rounds have been worked and 37 (45) sts remain on round.

Work a round from RS with 1 sl st in every st through both loops.
Break yarn and finish off.
Work the other sleeve in the same way.

FLOUNCE

Join yarn in 1st st at side by counting 12 (14) rows from beg of neckline.
The yoke hangs down as you work the flounce from top to bottom.

Row 1 (RS): On the 12th (14th) row of the yoke, work 2 ch, 2 htr FLO in every st until the last 4 sts (do not work the last 4 sts on the side where the buttons are sewn in – there should be room for overlap when buttoning the vest) (310 (358) sts). Turn.

Row 2: ch 2, 1 htr BLO in every st (310 (358) sts). Turn.

Rep row 2 until a total of 3 (4) rows have been worked on flounce.
Finish the flounce with a row of 1 sl st in every st.
Break yarn and finish off.

FINISHING

Weave in any remaining ends.
Sew on buttons (leave the rustic back of button visible if desired) using the colour of yarn you are working in. If the buttonholes are on the large side, tighten them with a single stitch.
Gently steam and press the vest under a dry cloth.

Anni's T-shirt

Mix and match this T-shirt with Peer Bo's sunhat and Anton's nappy pants, or with Karl Viggo's trousers. This makes a lovely summer set for baby. The T-shirt is worked top down in one piece with increases in a round yoke of half treble crochet rib. It is short in design and may be a little chunky. The T-shirt is buttoned at the neck.

Sizes
3 (6) 9 (12) 24 months

Measurements
Length: approx. 20 (24) 26 (28) 30cm
Chest width: approx. 40 (45) 50 (56) 62cm

Yarn
Sandnes Tynn Line, 53% cotton, 33% viscose and 14% linen, 220 metres/50g
Colour A: wheat 1015
Colour B: terracotta 3513
Quantity: 50 (50) 50 (100) 100g for colour A and 50g colour B (applies to all sizes)

Other materials
1 mother-of-pearl button: approx. 1.5cm in diameter

Crochet hook
3mm

Tension
27–28 htr BLO x 18 rounds = 10 x 10cm
24 dc x 30 rounds in colour pattern = 10 x 10cm

Note
Make sure that you work the very last st on a row; it can be difficult to find when working BLO.
Turning chains are not counted in the total stitch count.
Work the yoke with htr. However, the first 5 sts and the last 5 sts are dc rib to tighten up the edge.
Insert a stitch marker on RS of piece.
Make sure increases are evenly spaced on yoke and not made on top of each other from row to row so the edge is rounded and smooth not jagged.
See p. 19 for how to work spike stitches.

Pattern
On yoke and sleeves work all sts BLO from row 2 unless otherwise stated in pattern.

Pattern in the two-colour pattern is crocheted through both loops and not BLO.

When changing colour, pull the new colour yarn through sts at the beg of the round. Only then work the next stitch (as shown in pattern) with the new colour yarn. Make sure that the yarn not in use is brought up on WS of piece.

Two-colour pattern: divisible by 4 sts
Round 1 (RS): change to colour B. Ch 1, dc 1 in next 3 sts, *ch 2, skip 1 st, dc 1 in next 3 sts*, rep from * to * around. Finish round with 2 ch, skip 1 st, 1 sl st in 1st dc. Turn and work the opposite way.

Round 2: ch 1, dc in 1st st, *ch 2, skip ch-space, dc in next 3 sts*, rep from * to * around. Finish round with 2 ch, skip ch-space, and work 1 dc in each of the last 2 ch. Close round with 1 sl st in 1st dc. Turn.

Round 3 (RS): Change to colour A. Ch 1, *ch 1, ch 2, skip 1 st, ch 1 in next st, then work 1 spike stitch as follows: 1 tr around 2-ch space and straight down in st 3 rounds below*, rep from * to * around. Finish with 1 sl st in 1st dc. Turn.

Round 4: ch 1, dc 3, *ch 2, skip ch-space, dc 1 in next 3 sts*, rep from * to * around. Finish with 2 ch, skip ch-space, and close round with 1 sl st in 1st dc. Turn.

Round 5 (RS): Change to colour B. Ch 1, *1 dc in next st, then work 1 spike stitch as follows: 1 tr around 2-ch space and straight down in st on 2nd round; 1 dc, 2 ch, skip 1 st, *, rep from * to * around. Finish round with 1 sl st in 1st dc. Turn.

Round 6: ch 1, dc in 1st st *ch 2, skip ch-space, dc in next 3 sts*, rep from * to * around. Finish with 2 ch and skip ch-space, 1

dc in last 2 sts, and close round with 1 sl st in 1st dc. Turn.

Rep rounds 3–6, to measurements given in pattern below or to desired length. Finish the pattern with the following 2 rounds:

Round 7 (RS): change to colour A. * 1 dc in first 3 sts, then 1 spike stitch as follows: 1 tr around 2-ch spaces and straight down in st 3 rounds below*, rep from * to * around, ending with 1 dc in last 3 sts.

Round 8 (again from RS): 1 dc in every st around.

YOKE

Leave approx. 2 metres of yarn in colour A hanging at the beginning, which you will use to work slip stitch edging etc. in neckline. Work sl sts as soon as you can to avoid having to keep the yarn hanging during the rest of the work. This is done as follows: With the long end from the cast-on, work 1 sl st in every st from RS, work 5 ch for button loop, and fasten the loop with a few sl sts further down the slit.

Work 62 (68) 76 (82) 87 ch with colour A.

Row 1 (RS): 1 htr in 3rd ch from hook, 1 htr in every subsequent ch (60 (66) 74 (80) 85 sts). Turn.

Row 2: ch 1, dc 1 (remember to work BLO from now on) in first 5 sts, htr 1 and at the same time make 8 incs evenly spaced in next 50 (56) 64 (70) 75 sts, dc 1 in last 5 sts (68 (74) 82 (88) 93 sts). Turn.

Row 3: ch 1, dc 1 in the first 5 sts, htr 1 and at the same time make 8 incs evenly spaced in the next 58 (64) 72 (78) 83 sts, dc 1 in the last 5 sts (76 (82) 90 (96) 101 sts). Turn.

Row 4: ch 1, dc 1 in the first 5 sts, htr 1 and at the same time make 8 incs evenly spaced in the next 66 (72) 80 (86) 91 sts, dc 1 in the last 5 sts (84 (90) 98 (104) 109 sts). Turn.

Make sure that increases are not made on top of each other from row to row so the piece is smooth and rounded rather than jagged at the edges.

Rep row 4 until a total of 10 (12) 14 (15) 16 rows increase have been worked. There will be a total of 11 (13) 15 (16) 17 rows on yoke and 140 (162) 186 (200) 213 sts on row. Break yarn and finish off.

BODY

Cont working over sts in front and back sections. Divide sts by counting 20 (23) 27 (30) 32 sts (right back piece), 30 (35) 39 (40) 43 sts (sleeve stitches not worked), 40 (46) 54 (60) 63 sts (front piece), 30 (35) 39 (40) 43 sts (sleeve) and 20 (23) 27 (30) 32 sts (left back piece).
Place stitch markers between the pieces. The join is at the back of the left side of the T-shirt.

Work as usual through both loops and no longer BLO.

Round 1 (RS): start on left back piece and join yarn, ch 1, htr in first 20 (23) 27 (30) 32 sts, work directly across slits with htr in next 20 (23) 27 (30) 32 sts, (23) 27 (30) 32 sts on right back piece (vent is now closed), ch 5 (6) 8 (8) 10 in armhole, skip 30 (35) 39 (40) 43 sts, 1 htr in front piece 40 (46) 54 (60) 63 sts, 5 (6) 8 (8) 10 ch in armhole, skip last sleeve stitches, close round with 1 sl st in 1st htr, closing piece into a ring (90 (104) 124 (136) 147 sts).

Round 2 (again from RS): start two-colour pattern by following pattern 1st round. At the same time increase the number of stitches to fit the pattern (it is divisible by 4 sts) as follows: 2 (0) 0 (0) 1 dc (92 (104) 124 (136) 148 sts).

Continue working in pattern until body measures 19 (23) 25 (27) 29 cm or to desired length. Finish with rounds 7–8 in pattern. Work an edge of 1 sl st in every st from RS. Break yarn and finish off.

SHORT SLEEVES

Work sleeves with htr rib on every round. Start by attaching yarn in the middle of armhole. Remember that the pattern must fit so that you work BLO from the RS.

Anni's winter blouse, with Manna's moccasins (page 184) and Anton's nappy pants (page 76).

Round 1 (WS): insert yarn in the middle of armholes, work 2 ch, 1 htr in the same st, then 1 htr in the next ch, work 1 htr around the htr on last row on yoke, rather than into it (in this case the htr is in the horizontal position), work 1 htr in each of the 30 (35) 39 (40) 43 sts of sleeve, work again 1 htr around the htr on last row on yoke and finish with 1 htr in each of the last ch in armhole. Close round with 1 sl st in 1st htr through both loops (37 (43) 49 (50) 53 sts). Turn and work the other way around.

Round 2 (RS): 2 ch, 1 htr, dec 1, 1 htr in every st in the round. Close round (36 (42) 48 (49) 52 sts). Turn.

Rep round 2 until a total of 5 (6) 7 (8) 9 rounds have been worked and 33 (38) 43 (43) 45 sts remain on sleeve.

Work a round from RS with 1 sl st in every st through both loops.
Break yarn and finish off.
Work the other sleeve in the same way.

FINISHING
Weave in any remaining ends.
Sew button on slit at neck.
Steam and press the blouse under a dry cloth.

Tip

Work a winter jumper following the pattern for Anni's T-shirt, but use wool yarn (Sandnes Sunday is shown here in the colours brown sugar and dusty purple). Work two-colour pattern on 3.5mm hook, add 5cm to the length of the T-shirt and long sleeves following the pattern for Amanda's dress, p. 160.

Thit's sweater

Thit's sweater is soft and feathery. It is worked in one piece from top to bottom. There are increases in a round yoke in half treble crochet and a two-colour pattern on the lower part of the body. The sleeves are plain and worked from the yoke in the same rib pattern.

Size
6 (12) 18 (24) months

Measurements
Length: approx. 25 (30) 33 (36)cm
Chest width: approx. 45 (49) 56 (62)cm
Body width: approx. 58 (66) 72 (80)cm

Yarn
Cewec Tibet, 24% yak, 55% merino wool,
21% polyamide, 190 metres/25g
Colour A: 17 rust brown
Colour B: 25 pink
Quantity: 50 (75) 75 (100)g colour A, 25 (25)
50 (50)g colour B

Other materials
6 (7) 8 (9) mother-of-pearl buttons: approx.
1.5–2cm in diameter

Crochet hook
4mm

Tension
24 htr BLO x 16 rows = 10 x 10cm

20 dc x 26 rows in pattern = 10 x 10cm

Note
Make sure that you work the very last st
on a row; it can be difficult to find when
working BLO.
Turning chains are not counted in the total
stitch count.
Feel free to put a stitch marker on RS.
Make sure increases are evenly spaced on
the yoke and not made right on top of
each other from row to row so the piece is
rounded and not jagged on the edges.
See p. 19 for how to work spike stitches.
When changing colour, pull the new colour
through at the last pull-through on the last
st in the old colour. Make sure that the yarn
not in use is brought up to the WS of the
piece.

Pattern
All sts are worked BLO from row 2 unless
otherwise stated in pattern.
Two-colour pattern is not worked BLO but
through both loops

Two-colour pattern: divisible by 4 + 3 sts

Row 1 (RS): change to colour B. 1 dc in first 3 sts, *2 ch, skip 1 st, 1 dc in next 3 sts*, rep from * to * to end.

Row 2: 1 dc in first 3 sts, *2 ch, skip ch-space, 1 dc in next 3 sts*, rep from * to * to end.

Row 3 (RS): change to colour A. *1 dc, 2 ch, skip 1 st, 1 dc in next st, then work 1 spike stitch as follows: 1 tr around 2-ch space and straight down in st 3 rows below*, rep from * to * to end. Finish with 1 dc, 2 ch, skip 1 st, 1 dc.

Row 4: 1 dc, *2 ch, skip ch-space, 1 dc in next 3 sts*, rep from * to * to end. Finish with 2 ch, skip ch-space, 1 dc.

Row 5 (RS): change to colour B. *1 dc in next st, then work 1 spike stitch as follows: 1 tr around 2-ch space and straight down in st on 2nd row; 1 dc, 2 ch, skip 1 st*, rep from * to * to end. Omit last 2 ch on last repeat.

Row 6: ch 1, dc 1 in first 3 sts *ch 2, skip ch-space, dc 1 in next 3 sts*, rep from * to * to end.

Rep rows 3–6 until measurements indicated below or until desired length.
Finish pattern piece with the following 2 rows:

Row 7: Change to colour A. *1 dc in first 3 sts, then 1 spike stitch as follows: 1 tr around 2-ch space and straight down in idle st 3 rows below*, rep from * to * to end, ending with 1 dc in last 3 sts.

Row 8: Work 1 dc in every st in row.

Buttonholes
Work until 4 sts remain on round, ch 1, skip 1 st and work htr or dc in last 3 sts as indicated in pattern.
On next row work that st in ch-space.
Rep buttonhole on every 4th row on yoke and on every 8th row on body.

YOKE
Leave approx. 2 metres yarn in colour A hanging at beg, which you will use to work sl st edge on neckline. Work sl sts as soon as you can to avoid having the yarn hanging during the rest of the work. Work 1 sl st in every st from RS with the long end from cast-on.

Work 52 (58) 66 (72) ch.

Row 1 (RS): 1 htr in 3rd ch from hook, 1 htr in every subsequent ch (50 (56) 64 (70) sts). Turn.

Row 2: Ch 2, 1 htr (remember to work BLO) in every st, at the same time work 8 incs evenly spaced (in approximately every 5th (6th) 7th (8th) st), and work a buttonhole at the end of round (58 (64) 72 (78) sts). Turn.

Row 3: ch 2, htr 1 in every st, at the same time work 8 incs evenly spaced (in every 6th (7th) 8th (9th) st) (66 (72) 80 (86) sts). Turn.

Row 4: Ch 2, 1 htr in every st, at the same time work 8 incs evenly spaced (in every 7th (8th) 9th (10th) st) (74 (80) 88 (94) sts). Turn.

Rep row 4 and increase the number of stitches by 8 sts on every row 11 (13) 15 (17) times in total. NB: Remember one buttonhole on every 4th row. When the yoke has been worked, there are a total of 12 (14) 16 (18) rows and 138 (160) 184 (206) sts on row.
Do not break yarn but continue working separately on sleeves and body.

BODY
Divide piece by counting, preferably PM after each section, 24 (28) 31 (35) sts (front piece), 24 (28) 32 (36) sts (sleeve), 42 (48) 58 (64) sts (back piece), 24 (28) 32 (36) sts (sleeve) and 24 (28) 31 (35) sts (front piece).

Work regular dc in two-colour pattern, no longer BLO.

Row 1 (RS): ch 1, dc 1 in the first 24 (28) 31 (35) sts, skip 24 (28) 32 (36) sts, work 6 (6) 8 (8) ch in armhole, 1 dc in each of the next 42 (48) 58 (64) sts, skip 24 (28) 32 (36) sts, ch 6 (6) 8 (8) in armhole, 1 dc in last 24 (28) 31 (35) sts (total 102 (116) 136 (150) sts). Turn.

Row 2: ch 1, dc 1 in each st, work 13 (15) 7 (9) incs evenly (number of stitches now divisible by 4, incl. 3 + 12 sts for dc rib) (total 115 (131) 143 (159) sts). Turn.

Place an extra ball of yarn in colour A on the right side of the sweater to change to colour A in dc rib when working with colour B in pattern.

Row 3: Ch 1, 6 dc BLO with colour A, change to colour B and begin two-colour pattern by following 1st row of pattern. When 6 sts remain, work dc BLO with colour A (115 (131) 143 (159) sts). Turn.

Row 4: ch 1, 6 dc BLO with colour A. Follow 2nd row of two-colour pattern until 6 sts remain, in which work dc BLO and a buttonhole with colour A. (115 (131) 143 (159) sts). Turn.

Row 5: Ch 1, 6 dc BLO with colour A. Follow 3rd row of two-colour pattern until 6 sts remain, then work dc BLO with colour A. (115 (131) 143 (159) sts). Turn.

Row 6: ch 1, 6 dc BLO with colour A. Follow 4th row of two-colour pattern until 6 sts remain, then work dc BLO and a buttonhole with colour A. (115 (131) 143 (159) sts. Turn.

Continue two-colour pattern. Work the outermost 6 sts of each side in dc rib in colour A. Change colour first after and before dc rib. Rep buttonholes every 8th row on body until there are 6 (7) 8 (9) buttonholes in total.

Work pattern until sweater measures approx. 25 (30) 33 (36)cm or to desired length. Finish with rows 7–8 of the pattern. Work 2 more rows dc with colour A. Finish with a row of 1 sl st in every st from RS. Break yarn and finish off.

SLEEVES
Work sleeves with htr rib. Remember that rib pattern must fit so work BLO from the RS.

Round 1 (RS): join yarn in the middle of armhole, work 2 ch, 1 htr in same st, 1 htr in each of the next ch, work 1 htr around the htr on last row on yoke, rather than into it, 1 htr in each of the 24 (28) 32 (36) sts of sleeve, work again 1 htr around the htr on last row on yoke, and finish with 1 htr in each of the last ch in armhole. Close round with a sl st in 1st htr through both loops now and on remaining rounds on sleeve. (32 (36) 42 (46) sts). Turn and work the other way around.

Round 2 (WS): 2 ch, 1 htr in each st. Close round (32 (36) 42 (46) sts). Turn.

Round 3 (RS): ch 2, 1 htr in each st. Close round (32 (36) 42 (46) sts). Turn.

Rep rounds 2 and 3 until sleeve measures 18 (20) 24 (26)cm from armhole or to desired length. You can also work extra length of 5cm and make a small turn-up on the sleeve.
On last round, work 4 (5) 6 (7) decs for a total of 28 (31) 36 (39) sts. Then work from RS one round with 1 sl st in every st through both loops.
Break yarn and finish off.
Work the other sleeve the same way.

FINISHING
Weave in the last ends and sew on buttons. Gently steam and press the sweater under a dry cloth.

Tip

Lang Yarns Nova is a suitable yarn alternative for the sweater. Work with a 4.5mm hook, as this yarn is very elastic and contracts.

Eva's romper

Eva's romper is very useful and comfortable for a baby to wear in both summer and winter. The yarn is a cotton and cashmere blend. The design is crocheted in one piece from the bottom up; the pattern is half treble crochet rib. There are buttons at the bottom and the shoulder sections can be pushed aside at the top. The bodice is therefore open at both ends so that it is easy to put on and take off and it is easy to change the baby's nappy.

Size
(3) (9) (18) 24 months

Measurements
Length: approx. 29 (36) 40 (44)cm
Romper circumference: approx. 41 (46) 50 (55)cm

Yarn
Permin Elise 90% cotton and 10% cashmere, 115 metres/25g
Colour: black 881115
Quantity: 75 (100) 100 (125)g

Other materials
3 mother-of-pearl buttons: approx. 1.5cm in diameter
Elastic: 60–70cm long

Crochet hooks
2.5mm and 3mm

Tension
27 htr BLO x 18 rounds = 10 x 10cm

Note
Make sure you work the very last st on a row; it can be hard to find when working BLO.
Turning chains are not counted in the total stitch count.

Pattern
All sts are worked BLO from 2nd row/round unless otherwise stated in pattern.

BUTTON RIB

Start with dc rib and 2.5mm crochet hook. Leave a short yarn end so that you can later work an edge of sl sts along the 10 sts at the end.

Work 11 ch.

1 dc in 2nd ch from hook, 1 dc in every ch (10 sts). Turn.

Row 1: ch 1, dc 1 in every st (10 sts). Turn.

Rep row 2 until you have 18 (20) 22 (24) rows.
Finish with a row of 1 sl st in each of the 10 sts (3 buttons will be sewn on this rib later).

BACK PIECE

Change to 3mm hook.

Work up along side of dc rib as follows:

Row 1 (RS): ch 1, 5 dc, 8 (10) 12 (14) htr, 5 dc (total 18 (20) 22 (24) sts), which corresponds to 1 st per row in dc rib. Turn.

Place a stitch marker on RS of piece.

Row 2 (WS): ch 1, dc 1 in first 5 sts, htr 2 (inc) in next st, htr 1 in each st until 6 sts remain, htr 2 in next st (inc), dc 1 in last 5 sts (20 (22) 24 (26) sts). Turn.

The 5 dc on each side are worked in rib for the leg opening.

Rep row 2 until incs have made a total of 56 (62) 68 (74) sts on row and 19 (21) 23 (25) rows have been worked on piece from dc rib.

Break yarn and finish off.
Put piece aside and work lower part of front piece.

FRONT PIECE

Work the same button rib as on the back piece. However, work 3 buttonholes in this rib, as follows:
On 4th row work first buttonhole: 1 dc in first 4 sts, ch 2, skip 2 sts, 1 dc in last 4 sts. On next row work 2 dc in ch-space. Work 2nd buttonhole on 10th (11th) 12th (13th) row. Work 3rd buttonhole on 15th (17th) 19th (21st) row.

Continue working as for the back piece until 1st row.

Insert a stitch marker on RS of piece.

Work 3 (5) 7 (9) rows straight without increases but work as for the back piece: 5 dc in each side and 8 (10) 12 (14) htr in the middle.

When a total of 4 (6) 8 (10) rows have been worked on piece, work incs in leg opening as follows: rep row 2 for back piece 10 (12) 14 (16) times. There are now 38 (44) 50 (56) sts on one row.
Do not break the yarn.

BODY

Round 1 (RS): work dc and htr as indicated by previous rows on front piece, 9 ch (so front and back piece are now worked together), continue by working over the back piece from

Tip

You could add ruffles on the bottom. See the description in pattern for Anton's nappy pants, p. 80.

Tip

Feel free to use other yarn types: bamboo, linen and cotton are excellent for summer clothes, while wool is ideal for winter.

RS (as before with 5 dc on each end), work 9 ch again. Finally join back piece and front piece to form a ring with 1 sl st.
1st dc through both loops on front piece (total 112 (124) 136 (148) sts).

Turn and work the other way around – now and later on body.

Round 1 (WS): ch 1, work 1 dc in the 9 ch on each side, and otherwise as sts of previous round, close round with 1 sl st in 1st dc through both loops (112 (124) 136 (148) sts). Turn.

Round 2 (RS): ch 1, work dc and htr BLO as previously, close round with 1 sl st in 1st dc through both loops (112 (124) 136 (148) sts). Turn.

Rep rounds 2 and 3 until a total of 8 rounds have been worked on body with htr and dc BLO. There will be a small dc rib across the leg opening, which is above the 9 ch on front piece in each side. The join on the round is thus placed at the front of the left side of the romper – after the 9 ch, which are in continuation of the back piece.

Then work 22 (28) 30 (32) rounds of htr in every st.
Piece measures approx. 14 (17) 18 (19)cm from leg opening.

On next round, work a row of holes for the elastic: 2 ch, 1 htr in first 4 sts, *1 ch, skip 1 st, 1 htr in next 4 sts*, rep from * to * around.
On next round, work 1 htr in every st and ch-loop (112 (124) 136 (148) sts).
Do not break yarn, but continue to work on sl sts.

SHOULDERS
Insert a sl st in each side of bodice dividing front and back piece: front piece: 56 (62) 68 (74) sts; back piece: 56 (62) 68 (74) sts. Work the shoulders back and forth with dc rib, starting in BLO and FLO respectively in the middle of front piece.

SHOULDER 1
Row 1 (RS): Slip yarn BLO in 10th (10th) 11th (11th) st on front piece, work 1 ch, 1 dc in 38 (44) 48 (54) sts.

Row 2: ch 1, dc 1 (remember to work BLO) in every st until 2 sts remain, dec 1, (37 (43) 47 (53) sts). Turn.

Row 3: ch 1, dec 1, dc in every st to end, (36 (42) 46 (52) sts). Turn.

Rep rows 2 and 3 until 15 (15) 16 (17) sts remain.
Work 22 (30) 34 (38) rows in dc rib.
If possible, try the romper on the child and work the shoulder sections to the correct length.
Break the yarn and fasten off.

SHOULDER 2
Work the second shoulder piece with dc in FLO (the free stitch space) exactly the same 38 (44) 48 (54) sts from RS (work in front of the first shoulder).

FINISHING

Weave in remaining ends.
Sew buttons on rib at the bottom.
Thread a length of elastic through the holes
in the waistband and tie a knot in the left
side of the romper. Work sl sts from RS along
edge of pants piece, starting just after romper
shoulder stitches on right side.
At the same time work the shoulder sections
where you want them at the back. Count that
there is an equal number of sts on each side of
the shoulders on the back piece.
Place shoulder sections and back piece
together, WS to WS, and work sts tog 2 by 2
with sl sts through both layers.
Note: there is a visible join on the right side
of piece.
Finally steam and press the romper under a
dry cloth.

Row 1 (RS): join yarn in FLO, work 1 ch, 1
dc FLO in same st and in every st over (38
(44) 48 (54) sts). Turn.

Row 2: ch 1, dec 1, dc (remember to work
BLO) in every st over (37 (43) 47 (53) sts).
Turn.

Row 3: ch 1, dc 1 in each st until 2 sts remain,
dec 1 (36 (42) 46 (52) sts). Turn.

Rep rows 2 and 3 until 15 (15) 16 (17) sts
remain.
Then work 22 (30) 34 (38) rows in dc rib or
the length of the first shoulder.
Break yarn and fasten off.

Alexander's bodysuit

This useful bodysuit is crocheted in Sandnes Alpaca Silk, which is a lovely soft yarn blend for a baby. The pattern is in double crochet rib. Choose whether you want short or long sleeves. A tiny ruffle at the neckline is also an option. The bodysuit has an unusual construction: it is worked from the top down and from the bottom up to create ribbing and buttons at the bottom. There is a slit and a button at the neck, and elastic is pulled through at the waist.

Size
3 (6) 12 (24) months

Measurements
Length: 31 (33) 35 (37)cm
Inseam: approx. 41 (46) 50 (55)cm

Yarn
Sandnes Alpaca Silk, 70% baby alpaca and 30% mulberry silk, 200 metres/50g
Colour: petrol blue 7572
Quantity: 150 (150) 200 (200)g (for long-sleeve version)

Other materials
4 buttons: approx. 1.5cm in diameter
Elastic: 60–70cm long

Crochet hooks
2.5mm and 3mm

Tension
27 htr BLO x 18 rounds = 10 x 10cm

Note
The upper part of the body is worked top down and then put aside. Then the lower section is worked from the bottom up. Finally the body top and bottom are joined together at the waist and the sleeves are added.

Make sure you work the very last st on a row; it can be hard to find when working BLO.

Turning chains are not counted in the total stitch count.

On the yoke, work htr – however, the first 5 sts and the last 5 sts are dc, to support the slit at the back.

Mark the raglan increases with stitch markers as explained in pattern.

Let the stitch markers (preferably yarn in a contrasting colour) be carried forward for each row.

The first inc of the two worked around the stitch marker is worked in st just above the stitch marker.

Pattern
Work all sts BLO from row 2 unless otherwise stated in pattern.

YOKE

Leave approx. 2 metres of yarn up to yarn end – this will be used to work a sl st in every st along neck edge from RS. Work sl sts as soon as you can to avoid having the long yarn end hanging during the rest of the work. Continue after sl sts to work a loop (for button) of 5 ch, fastening with a few sl sts a little further down the slit.

Work 71 (77) 83 (87) ch with 3mm hook.

Row 1 (RS): 1 dc in 2nd ch from hook, 1 dc in every subsequent ch (70 (76) 82 (86) dc). Turn.
If desired, insert a stitch marker on RS.
If you don't want to make the ruffle, skip next section and go to row 2.

Ruffle at neck edge (optional)
Row 1 (WS): ch 2, htr BLO 2 times in every st (140 (152) 164 (172) sts).

Turn with 1 ch and work from RS an edge with 1 sl st in each htr through both loops.
Break yarn and fasten off.
Continue from row 2 by joining yarn in 1st dc.

Row 2 (RS): ch 1, dc 1 BLO every st to end (70 (76) 82 (86) sts). Turn.
Row 3 (WS): ch 1, dc 1 BLO in every st (70 (76) 82 (86) dc). Turn. Then work again on yoke from 3rd row of pattern.

White and denim blue Sandnes Alpaca Silk. Bodysuit is worked in size 3 months, using one ball in each colour.

Row 2 (WS): ch 1, dc 1 in every st in row. Turn.

Now prepare to make the raglan shaping in 4 diagonal lines on RS.

Row 3 (RS): ch 1, dc 5, 6 (8) 9 (9) htr (back piece), fan inc (see p. 19), PM, fan inc, 9 (9) 10 (11) htr (sleeve), fan inc, PM, fan inc, 22 (24) 26 (28) htr (front piece), fan inc, PM, fan inc, 9 (9) 10 (11) htr (sleeve), fan inc, PM, fan inc, 6 (8) 9 (9) htr, 5 dc (back piece) (86 (92) 98 (102) sts). Turn.

Row 4 (WS): ch 1, dc 5, htr 1 in every st in row (86 (92) 98 (102) sts). Turn.

Row 5 (RS): ch 1, dc 5, 7 (9) 10 (10) htr, fan inc, slip marker, fan inc, 11 (11) 12 (13) htr, fan inc, slip marker, fan inc, 24 (26) 28 (30) htr, fan inc, slip marker, fan inc, 11 (11) 12 (13) htr, fan inc, slip marker, fan inc, 7 (9) 10 (10) htr, 5 dc (102 (108) 114 (118) sts). Turn.

Rep rows 4 and 5 until raglan is increased a total of 6 (7) 8 (9) times. Finish with a row 4. For fan inc, increase by 2 sts at beg and end (at slits) and 4 sts between inc rows. There are a total of 166 (188) 210 (230) sts on row divided into 24 (27) 31 (34) sts (back), 35 (39) 44 (48) sts (sleeve), 48 (54) 60 (66) sts (front), 35 (39) 44 (48) sts (sleeve) and 24 (27) 31 (34) sts (back). Break yarn and fasten off.

BODY OF BODICE

Divide sts on yoke as explained below so that sleeves can be finished separately and body can now be worked in the round and finished in one piece.

Round 1 (RS): insert yarn in 1st st on back piece, work 2 ch – this is just after sleeve stitches – 1 htr in 24 (27) 31 (34) sts (back piece), close slit at the back by working 1 htr in

Tip

You can work the top in one colour of yarn and the bottom in another colour. Tone on tone could also look effective.

the next 24 (27) 31 (34) sts (back piece – this is 1st st of yoke), skip 35 (39) 44 (48) sts (sleeve), 4 (6) 8 (8) ch (sleeve yoke), 1 htr in 48 (54) 60 (66) sts (front piece), skip again 35 (39) 44 (48) sts (sleeve), 4 (6) 8 (8) ch (armhole). Close round to form a ring with 1 sl st in 1st htr through both loops (104 (120) 138 (150) sts). Turn and work the opposite way.

Round 2: Ch 2, 1 htr in every st. Work 8 incs (4 inc) 2 dec (1 dec) evenly on round. Close round with 1 sl st in 1st htr (112 (124) 136 (148) sts). Turn.

Stitch count must match stitch count on bottom piece as body will be joined together here.

Round 3: Ch 2, 1 htr in every st. Close round with 1 sl st (112 (124) 136 (148) sts). Turn.

Rep round 3 until bodice measures approx. 5 (7) 8 (9)cm from armhole.

From RS work a round with holes for elastic: ch 2, *1 htr in next 4 sts through both loops, ch 1, skip 1 st* rep from * to * round. Close round with 1 sl st in 1st htr. Turn.

Work next round from WS: 2 ch, 1 htr BLO in every st and 1 htr in ch-spaces (112 (124) 136 (148) sts).
Do not break yarn. Put piece aside.

BUTTON RIB

Start with a dc rib and 2.5mm hook. Leave a 20cm yarn end, so you can later work a border of sl sts along the 10 sts at the end.

Work 11 ch.

Row 1: 1 dc in 2nd ch from hook, 1 dc in every ch to end (10 sts). Turn.

Row 2: ch 1, dc 1 in every st (10 sts). Turn.

Rep row 2 until a total of 18 (20) 22 (24) rows.
Finish with a row of sl sts in each of the 10 sts on both sides of rib. Do not break yarn.

Later sew 3 buttons on this piece of rib.

BACK PIECE

Change to 3mm crochet hook.
Work up along side of dc rib as follows:

Row 1 (RS): ch 1, 5 dc, 8 (10) 12 (14) htr, 5 dc (total 18 (20) 22 (24) sts), which corresponds to 1 st per row in dc rib. Turn.

Place a sl st on RS of piece.

Row 2: ch 1, dc 1 in first 5 sts, 2 htr (inc) in next st, 1 htr in every st until 6 sts remain, 2

Tip

You could crochet a ribbon to use instead of the waist tie.

Use the same yarn as for body and work approx. 180–200 ch. Work 1 htr in 3rd ch, 1 sl st in each of the next ch until last st, 1 htr in last st.

Finish off and fasten ends.

htr in next st (inc), dc 1 in last 5 sts (20 (22) 24 (26) sts). Turn.
The 5 dc on each side are worked in rib for the leg opening.

Rep row 2 until there are a total of 56 (62) 68 (74) sts on row and a total of 19 (21) 23 (25) rows have been worked on piece from dc rib. Break yarn and finish off.
Put piece aside and work bottom part of front piece.

FRONT PIECE
Work the same rib as on the back piece. However, work 3 buttonholes in this rib, as follows:

On row 4 work first buttonhole: 1 dc in first 4 sts, ch 2, skip 2 sts, 1 dc in last 4 sts. On next row work 2 dc in ch-space. Work next buttonhole on 10th (11th) 12th (13th) row. Work the last buttonhole on the 15th (17th) 19th row (21st) row.

Continue working as described on back piece up to and including 1st row.
Insert a stitch marker on RS of piece.
Then work 3 (5) 7 (9) rows without incs. Remember to work rib pattern with the same stitch distribution as on 1st row of back piece: 5 dc in each side and 8 (10) 12 (14) htr in the middle.

When 4 (6) 8 (10) rows have been worked, begin incs in leg opening as follows:
Work and rep row 2 of back piece for a total of 10 (12) 14 (16) times. There are now 38 (44) 50 (14) repetitions on front piece. (56) sts in total on front piece.

BODY OF BOTTOM PIECE
Round 1 (RS): work dc and htr as established on front piece, 9 ch (front and back piece are now worked together), continue.

Continue to work over back piece sts from RS (as sts show), work 9 ch again. Finally join back piece and front piece into a ring with 1 sl st in 1st dc through both loops on front piece (total (112 (124) 136 (148) sts). Turn and work the other way around now and when working on the rest of the body.

Round 2 (WS): ch 1, work 1 dc in the 9 ch, on each side, and otherwise as established, close round with 1 sl st in 1st dc through both loops (112 (124) 136 (148) sts). Turn.

Round 3 (RS): ch 1, work dc and htr BLO, as established, close round with 1 sl st in 1st dc through both loops (112 (124) 136 (148) sts). Turn.

Rep rounds 2 and 3 until a total of 8 rounds have been worked on body with htr and dc BLO as established. There will be a small dc rib across the leg opening, which is above the 9 ch on front piece on each side. The join on round is thus placed at the front of the body on the left side in continuation of the 9 ch after back piece.

Then work 24 (28) 30 (32) rounds straight with htr ch in every st. The piece measures approx. 15 (16) 17 (18)cm from leg opening. Break yarn and finish off.

JOIN UPPER PART AND LOWER PART
Insert a stitch marker in the side of the bodice and bottom to show exactly which sts belong to front piece and back piece. Follow sts in a straight line down from each armhole and place stitch marker. Follow sts in a straight line from the first and last sts on the back piece and slip st in place as follows.

Make sure the pieces are on top of each other, WS to WS. The top and bottom must not rotate away from each other. There are a total of 112 (124) 136 (148) sts on each piece.

Continue working with yarn from the top. Work sts together with sl sts from RS, 2 and 2, and through 2 layers.

The stitches are visible from the RS and must not be too tight. If necessary, use a crochet hook a half or full size larger.
Break the yarn and fasten off.

SHORT SLEEVES

Work sleeves with htr rib on 3mm hook. Start by attaching yarn in the middle of the sleeve yoke. Remember that the pattern must fit so that you work BLO from the RS.

Round 1 (RS): Attach yarn in the middle of the armhole, 2 ch, 1 htr in the same st, 1 htr in each of the next ch, work 1 htr around the htr on the last row on yoke, rather than into it (in this case the htr will be in the horizontal position), 1 htr in each of the 35 (39) 44 (48) sts of sleeve, work again 1 htr around the htr on last row on yoke, 1 htr in each of the last ch in armhole. Close round with 1 sl st in 1st htr now and in the future (41 (47) 54 (58) sts). Turn and work the other way round.

Round 2: ch 2, 1 htr in every st around, but work 1 dec where you worked around (rather than into) the htr in round 1. Close round with 1 sl st in 1st htr (39 (45) 52 (56) sts). Turn.

Round 3: Ch 2, 1 htr in next st, dec 1, 1 htr in each st, close round with 1 sl st in 1st htr (38 (44) 51 (55) sts). Turn.

Rep round 3, 5 (7) 8 (9) times in total with a single dec (i.e. 7 (9) 10 (11) rounds in total on sleeve). There are 34 (38) 44 (45) sts left on sleeve. Now work from RS – not tightly – an edge on sleeve with sl sts as follows: work 1 sl st in every st through both loops. Alternatively, you can make a picot or crab stitch edging (see p. 31).

Break yarn and finish off.
Work the other sleeve in the same way.

LONG SLEEVES

Work as described under short sleeves up to and including round 2.

Round 3: 2 ch, 1 htr in every st, finish with 1 sl st in 1st htr (39 (45) 52 (56) sts). Turn.

Rep round 3 until sleeve is the correct length. Work an inc at beg and end of a round when the sleeve measures approx. 5, 10 and 15cm (after inc 33 (39) 46 (50) sts remain).

Work until sleeve measures approx. 15 (20) 23 (26)cm from armhole or to desired length. If necessary, work extra length for a small turn-up so that sleeves can grow a little with the child. On last round, work 5 (6) 7 (7) decs evenly (28 (33) 39 (43) sts).
From RS work one round with 1 sl st in every st through both loops.
Break yarn and finish off. Work the other sleeve the same way.

FINISHING

Weave in remaining ends. Work sl sts on dc rib with yarn end.
Insert a length of elastic in the waist, adjust the size, and tie a knot in the front of the belly.
Sew button at neck.
Steam and press the piece under a dry cloth.

Tip

Two ruffles can be worked on the bottom. Follow the instructions in the pattern for Anton's nappy pants, p. 80.

Emmy's dress

The pattern for the top of Alexander's bodysuit is used as the basis for this cute dress. Work the fine ruffle into the neck edge and pull a length of elastic between stitches at the bottom of the yoke.

Cashmere Blend from Fru Krogh in a powder pink colour (hand-dyed yarn) of baby alpaca, cashmere, silk and merino, 400 metres/100g

Quantity: 150 (150) 200 (250)g (for short sleeves)

Work according to pattern for bodysuit on p. 140. Work the small ruffle at the neck edge. After yoke piece, work fan increase (p. 19) in every 4th st on 1st round of body from RS.

There are now approx. 156 (180) 207 (225) sts on body.
Continue working straight with htr BLO on body stitches. Work until dress measures approx. 28 (32) 39 (44)cm or desired length or until there is no yarn left.
Finish edge from RS using crab stitch, slip stitches or picot stitches (see p. 31).

Agnes Marie's Christmas dress

This dress is worked in a light and elastic yarn with camel fibres and merino wool. The yarn produces a less pronounced stitch pattern, resulting in a completely different look in comparison to Amanda's dress, p. 156. There is a half treble crochet rib on the sleeves and yoke and a two-colour crochet pattern on the bottom of the dress. This dress is worked relatively quickly with a 4.5mm hook and is my idea of a nice Christmas dress.

Size
6 (12) 18 (24) months

Measurements
Length: 34 (38) 42 (46)cm
Chest width: 43 (49) 56 (63)cm
Dress width: approx. 60–90cm

Yarn
Lang Yarns Nova, 48% merino wool, 32% camel, and 20% polyamide, 180 metres/25g
Colour A: aubergine 080
Colour B: light grey 096
Quantity: 75 (75) 75 (100)g colour A, 25 (50) 50 (75)g colour B

Other materials
Length of elastic for yoke 60–70cm
1 mother-of-pearl button: 1.5–2cm in diameter

Crochet hook
4.5mm

Tension
20 htr BLO x 14 rows = 10 x 10cm
18 dc x 24 rows in two-colour pattern = 10 x 10cm

Note
Make sure that you work the very last st on a row; it can be difficult to find when working BLO.
Insert a stitch marker on RS of piece.
Turning chains are not counted in total stitch count.

On all rows in yoke work first 5 sts and last 5 sts as dc to support the slit.
See p. 19 for how to work spike stitches.

When changing colour, pull the new colour through at beg of round. Only then work a new stitch (as shown in pattern) with the new colour of yarn. Make sure the yarn not in use is brought up on the WS of the piece.

Pattern
On yoke and sleeves work all sts BLO from row 2 unless otherwise stated in pattern.
Do not work two-colour pattern BLO.

Two-colour pattern: divisible by 4 sts
Round 1 (RS): change to colour B. Ch 1, dc
1 in next 3 sts, *ch 2, skip 1 st, dc 1 in next 3
sts*, rep from * to * around. Finish round with
2 ch, skip 1 st, 1 sl st in 1st dc. Turn piece (and
work the opposite way).

Round 2 (WS): ch 1, dc 1 in 1 st, *ch 2, skip
2-ch space, 1 dc in next 3 sts*, rep from * to
* around. Finish round with 2 ch, skip 2-ch
space, 1 dc in each of the last 2 sts. Close
round with 1 sl st in 1st dc. Turn.

Round 3 (RS): Change to colour A. Ch 1, *ch
1, dc 2, skip 1 st, dc 1 in next st, then work
spike stitch as follows: 1 tr around 2-ch space
and straight down in st 3 rows below*, rep
from * to * round. Finish with 1 sl st in 1st dc.
Turn.

Round 4 (WS): ch 1, dc 3, ch *2, skip 2-ch
space, dc 1 in next 3 sts*, rep from * to *
around. Finish with 2 ch, skip 2-ch space, and
close round with 1 sl st in 1st dc. Turn.

Round 5 (RS): Change to colour B. Ch 1, then
*1 dc in next st, then work spike stitch as
follows: 1 tr around 2-ch space and straight
down in st on round 2; 1 dc, 2 ch, skip 1 st*,
rep from * to * around. Finish round with 1 sl
st in 1st dc. Turn.

Round 6 (WS): ch 1, dc 1 in 1st st, *ch 2, skip
2-ch space, dc 1 in next 3 sts*, rep from * to *
around. Finish with 2 ch, skip 2-ch space, 1 dc
in last 2 sts, and close round with 1 sl st in 1st
dc. Turn.

Rep rounds 3–6 to measurements given in
pattern below, or to desired length.

Finish pattern with the following 2 rounds:
Round 7 (RS): change to colour A. * 1 dc in
first 3 sts, then a spike stitch as follows: 1 tr
around 2-ch space and straight down in st 3
rounds below*, rep from * to * around, ending
with 1 dc in last 3 sts.

Round 8 (again from RS): 1 dc in every st
around.

YOKE

Leave approx. 2 metres of yarn in colour A
hanging at beg, which you will use to work sl
sts in neckline. Work sl sts as soon as you can
to avoid having the yarn hanging during the
rest of the work. This is done as follows:
With the long end from the cast-on, work 1 sl
st in every st from RS, work 5 ch for button
loop, and fasten the loop with a few sl sts
further down the slit.

Work 62 (68) 76 (82) ch.

Row 1 (RS): 1 htr in 3rd ch from hook, 1 htr
in every subsequent ch (60 (66) 74 (80) sts).
Turn.

Row 2: ch 1, dc in first 5 sts (remember to
work BLO from row 2) htr 1 in the next 50
(56) 64 (70) sts, and at the same time 8 incs
evenly spaced, dc 1 in the last 5 sts (68 (74)
82 (88) sts). Turn.

Row 3: ch 1, dc 1 in the first 5 sts, htr 1 in the
next 58 (64) 72 (78) sts, and at the same time
8 incs evenly spaced, dc 1 in the last 5 sts (76
(82) 90 (96) sts). Turn.

Row 4: ch 1, dc 1 in the first 5 sts, htr 1 in the
next 66 (72) 80 (86) sts, and at the same time
8 incs evenly spaced, dc 1 in the last 5 sts (84
(90) 98 (104) sts). Turn.

Make sure that the increases are not made
on top of each other from row to row so the
piece is rounded at the edge, not jagged.

Tip

*Cewec Tibet Yak is a very fine and light
yarn alternative for the dress, but use a
4mm hook as this yarn is somewhat less
elastic.*

Rep until you have a total of 10 (12) 14 (15) rows with increases. There will be a total of 11 (13) 15 (16) rows on yoke and 140 (162) 186 (200) sts on row.
Break yarn and finish off.

LOWER PART OF DRESS WITH PATTERN

Continue to work on round over sts of front piece and back piece.
Divide the sts by counting 20 (23) 25 (28) sts (right back piece), 30 (35) 42 (44) sts (sleeve sts not worked), 40 (46) 52 (56) sts (front piece), 30 (35) 42 (44) sts (sleeve) and 20 (23) 25 (28) sts (left back piece).
The join for the round is at the back of the left side of the dress. Work through both loops from now on and no longer BLO.

Round 1 (RS): Start at left back piece and join yarn, work 2 ch, 1 htr through both loops in first 20 (23) 25 (28) sts, work directly across the slit with 1 htr in next 20 (23) 25 (28) sts, (23) 25 (28) sts on right back piece, 5 (6) 8 (10) ch in armhole, skip 30 (35) 42 (44) sts, work 1 htr in front piece 40 (46) 52 (56) sts, ch 5 (6) 8 (10) in armholes, skip the last sleeve stitches, close round with 1 sl st in 1st htr, closing piece into a ring (90 (104) 118 (132) sts).

Round 2 (again on RS): ch 2, *1 htr in next 3 sts, fan inc (see p. 19) in next st*, rep from * to * round. Close round with 1 sl st in 1st htr (136 (156) 176 (196) sts). If necessary, adjust the number of stitches to fit the two-colour pattern on next round.

Round 3: Begin pattern.

Work pattern straight until piece measures 30 (34) 38 (42)cm or work to desired length.
Calculate 4–5cm extra edge.
Finish with round 7–8 of pattern.

Work 5 rounds htr rib in colour A.
Finally work 1 round with 1 sl st in every st through both loops from RS.
Break yarn and cast off.

SHORT SLEEVES

Work sleeves with htr rib.
Start by attaching yarn in the middle of armhole. Remember that the pattern must fit so that you work BLO from the RS.

Round 1 (WS): Attach yarn in the middle of armhole, work 2 ch, 1 htr in same st, then 1 htr in each of the next ch, work 1 htr around the htr on last row on yoke, rather than into it, 1 htr in each of the 30 (35) 42 (44) sts of sleeve, work again 1 htr around the htr staff from last row on yoke, and finish with 1 htr in each of the last ch in armhole. Close round with 1 sl st in 1st htr through both loops (37 (43) 52 (56) sts). Turn and work the other way around.

Round 2 (RS): 2 ch, 1 htr, dec 1, 1 htr in every st in the round. Close round (36 (42) 51 (55) sts). Turn.

Rep round 2, alternating from RS and WS, until a total of 5 (6) 7 (8) rounds have been worked. There are 33 (38) 46 (49) sts remain on round.

Work a round from RS with 1 sl st in every st through both loops.
Break yarn and finish off.
Work the other sleeve the same way.

LONG SLEEVES

Work as described under short sleeves. On round 2, however, work a decrease where an extra htr was worked on round 1 (in both sides at transition between armhole and sleeve stitches).

Do not work any more decs on sleeve.
Instead, work straight until sleeve measures
18 (21) 23 (26)cm from armhole or to desired
length.
On last round work 4 (5) 6 (7) decs. Then
work a round from RS with 1 sl st in every st
through both loops.
Break yarn and finish off.
Work the other sleeve the same way.

FINISHING

Weave in any remaining ends, and sew a
button on the neck slit. If desired, gently
pull a length of elastic in and out at intervals
of 4–5 stitches at the bottom of the yoke to
adjust the dress for each child.
Gently steam and press the dress under a
dry cloth.

Amanda's dress

*Tynn Line from Sandnes is a soft yarn combining linen, cotton and viscose,
so the dress falls beautifully with a certain heaviness. Pair the dress with
Peer Bo's sunhat, Anton's nappy pants or Manna's moccasins. The dress is
worked top down in one piece, with increases in a round yoke of half treble
crochet rib. The dress is buttoned at a slit at the neck.*

Sizes
Size: 3 (6) 9 (12) 24 months

Measurements
Length: 28 (33) 38 (42) 46cm
Chest width: 33 (39) 46 (50) 54cm
Skirt width: 57 (65) 76 (85) 90cm

Yarn
Sandnes Tynn Line, 53% cotton, 33% viscose
and 14% linen, 220 metres/50g
Colour A: chalky 1015
Colour B: blue-grey 6061
Quantity: 100 (150) 150 (150) 200g colour
A, 50 (100) 100 (100) 150g colour B

Other materials
Length of elastic for yoke 60–70cm
1 mother-of-pearl button: approx. 1.5cm
in diameter

Crochet hook
3mm

Tension
27 htr BLO x 18 rounds = 10 x 10cm

24 dc x 30 rounds in two-colour pattern =
10 x 10cm

Note
Make sure that you work the very last st
on a row; it can be difficult to find when
working BLO.
Turning chains are not counted in total
stitch count.
Place a stitch marker on RS of piece.
On all rows in yoke, work first 5 sts and last
5 sts as dc to support the slit.

See p. 19 for how to work spike stitches.

When changing colour, pull the new colour
through at beg of round. Only then work
a new stitch (as shown in pattern) with the
new colour yarn. Make sure the yarn not in
use is brought up on the WS of the piece.

Pattern
On yoke and sleeves work all sts BLO from
2nd row unless otherwise stated in pattern.
Two-colour pattern is not worked BLO.

Colour pattern: divisible by 4 sts

Round 1 (RS): change to colour B. Ch 1, dc 1 in next 3 sts, *ch 2, skip 1 st, dc 1 in next 3 sts*, rep from * to * around.
Finish round with 2 ch, skip 1 st, 1 sl st in 1st dc. Turn piece (and work the opposite way).

Round 2: ch 1, dc 1 in 1st st, ch 2, skip 2-ch space, dc 1 in next 3 sts*, rep from * to * around. Finish round with 2 ch, skip 2-ch space, and work 1 dc in each of the last 2 sts. Turn.

Round 3: Change to colour A. Ch 1, *ch 1, dc 2, skip 1 st, dc 1 in next st, then work spike stitch as follows: tr 1 around 2-ch space and straight down in st 3 rounds below*, rep from * to * around. Finish with 1 sl st in 1st dc. Turn.

Round 4: ch 1, dc 3, *ch 2, skip 2-ch space, dc 1 in next 3 sts*, rep from * to * around. Finish with ch 2, skip 2-ch space, and close round with 1 sl st in 1st dc. Turn.

Round 5: Change to colour B. Ch 1, *1 dc in (first) st, then work spike stitch as follows: 1 tr around 2-ch space and straight down in st 3 rounds below; ch 1, dc 2, skip 1 st*, rep from * to * around. Finish round with 1 sl st in 1st dc. Turn.

Round 6: ch 1, dc 1 in 1st st, *ch 2, skip 2-ch space, dc 1 in next 3 sts*, rep from * to * around. Finish with 2 ch and skip 2-ch loop, 1 dc in last 2 sts, and close round with 1 sl st in 1st dc. Turn.

Rep rounds 3–6 to measurements given in pattern below to desired length.

Finish the pattern with the following 2 rounds:
Round 7 (RS): change to colour A. * 1 dc in first 3 sts, then work as follows: 1 tr around 2-ch space and straight down in st 3 rounds below*, rep from * to * around, ending with 1 dc in last 3 sts.

Round 8 (again from RS): 1 dc in every st around.

YOKE

Leave approx. 2 metres yarn in colour A hanging at beg, which you will use to sl st neckline.
Work sl sts as soon as you can to avoid having the yarn hanging during the rest of the work. Work 1 sl st in every st from RS with the long end from the cast-on, work 5 ch for the button loop and fasten the button loop with a few sl sts further down in the slit.

Work 62 (68) 76 (82) 87 ch with colour A.

Row 1 (RS): 1 htr in 3rd ch from hook, 1 htr in every subsequent ch (60 (66) 74 (80) 85 sts). Turn.

Row 2: 1 htr in the next 50 (56) 64 (70) 75 sts and at the same time 8 incs evenly spaced, 1 dc in the last 5 sts (68 (74) 82 (88) 93 sts). Turn.

Row 3: 1 htr in the next 58 (64) 72 (78) 83 sts and at the same time 8 incs evenly spaced, 1 dc in the last 5 sts (76 (82) 90 (96) 101 sts). Turn.

Row 4: 1 htr in the next 66 (72) 80 (86) 91 sts and at the same time 8 incs evenly spaced, 1 dc in the last 5 sts (84 (90) 98 (104) 109 m). Turn.

Make sure that the increases are not made on top of each other from row to row to keep the edge rounded instead of jagged.

Rep increases until there is a total of 10 (12) 14 (15) 16 rows with increases. Increase by 2 sts between rows. At the beg and end of a row inc 1 st before and after an increase. There are now a total of 11 (13) 15 (16) 17 rows on yoke and 140 (162) 186 (200) 213 sts on piece.
Break yarn and cast off.

*Amanda's dress in size 24 months, where Colour A is navy blue and
Colour B is crocheted with yarn scraps in different colours.*

BOTTOM PART OF THE DRESS WITH PATTERN

Continue to work on round over front and back sts. Divide the sts by counting and placing the markers as follows: 20 (23) 27 (30) 32 sts (right back piece), 30 (35) 39 (40) 43 sts (sleeve sts, not worked), 40 (46) 54 (60) 63 sts (front piece), 30 (35) 39 (40) 43 (sleeve) and 20 (23) 27 (30) 32 sts (left back piece). Work dc in the normal way and no longer BLO. The join is at the back of the left side of the dress before left back.

Round 1 (RS): start on left back sts, join yarn, ch 1, 1 htr in first 20 (23) 27 (30) 32 sts, work directly across the slit with 1 htr in next 20 (23) 27 (30) 32 sts. (23) 27 (30) 32 sts on right back piece (slit is now closed), ch 5 (6) 8 (8) 10 in armhole, skip 30 (35) 39 (40) 43 sts, 1 htr in front piece 40 (46) 54 (60) 63 sts, 5 (6) 8 (8) 10 ch in armhole, skip armhole stitches again and close round with 1 sl st in 1st htr, closing piece into a ring (90 (104) 124 (136) 147 sts).

Round 2 (again on RS): 2 ch, *1 htr in next 3 sts, fan inc (see p. 19) in next st*, rep from * to * around. Close round with 1 sl st in 1st htr (136 (156) 184 (204) 220 sts).

Make sure the number of stitches is correct as the pattern is divisible by 4 sts.

Round 3: Begin colour pattern. Continue to use 3mm hook.

Work pattern until dress measures approx. 27 (32) 37) 41 (46)cm or work to desired length. Finish with round 7–8 in pattern.
Work an edge from RS: 1 sl st in every st through both loops. Break yarn and finish off.

SHORT SLEEVES

Work sleeves with htr rib. Start by attaching yarn in the middle of sleeve yoke at armhole. Remember that the pattern must fit so that you work BLO from the RS.

Round 1: insert yarn in middle of armhole, work 2 ch, 1 htr in same st, then 1 htr in each of the next ch, work 1 htr around the htr on the last row of yoke, rather than into it (in this case the htr will be in the horizontal position), 1 htr in each of the 30 (35) 39 (40) 43 sts, work again 1 htr around the htr on last row on yoke and finish with 1 htr in each of the last ch in armhole. Close round with 1 sl st in 1st htr through both loops (37 (43) 49 (50) 53 sts). Turn and work the other way around.

Round 2: 2 ch, 1 htr, dec 1, 1 htr in every st in the round. Close round (36 (42) 48 (49) 52 sts). Turn.

Rep round 2 until a total of 5 (6) 7 (8) 9 rounds. 33 (38) 43 (43) 45 sts remain on round.

Work a round from RS with 1 sl st in every st through both loops.
Break yarn and finish off.
Work the other sleeve the same way.

LONG SLEEVES

Work as described under short sleeves. On round 2, however, work an inc where an extra htr was worked on 1st round (on both sides at the transition between armhole and sleeve stitches). Total 35 (41) 47 (48) 51 sts. Do not work in front. Instead, work straight down until sleeve measures 15 (20) 23 (24)

25cm from armhole or to desired length. On last round work 4 (5) 6 (7) 7 evenly spaced decs (31 (36) 41 (41) 44 sts). Then work a round from RS with 1 sl st in every st through both loops.
Break yarn and finish off.
Work the other sleeve the same way.

FINISHING

Weave in any remaining ends and sew a button at the neck.
Carefully pull a length of elastic between sts at the bottom of the yoke at intervals of 4–5 stitches to adjust the dress to fit each child.
Steam and press the dress under a dry cloth.

Tip

Work Amanda's dress in wool and with long sleeves. Just make sure you crochet the weaving pattern on a 3.5mm hook. Try using Gründl Hot Socks Pearl superwash, 75% merino wool, 20% polyamide, 5% cashmere, 200m/50g, in Colour A: powder pink 19 and Colour B: raw white 01: you'll need 100 (150) 150 (150) 200g for Colour A and 50 (100) 100 (100) 150g for Colour B.

Tip

You can choose to crochet a crab stitch edge or a picot edge at the bottom of the dress and possibly on the sleeves too (see p. 31).

You can also work to 5cm before the measurements of the dress and finish with colour A as follows: 8 rounds with htr rib. Or you can choose to work a peplum, as on Milla's blouse, p. 47.

Leo's christening gown

Crochet a beautiful christening gown in Elise yarn by Permin in a blend of cotton and cashmere and Gepard's 100% linen to create some contrast and weight in the skirt, which has a lacy crochet pattern. Linen is a little stiff to crochet with, but it becomes soft and fine when washed. The christening gown is basically a longer version of Amanda's dress, p. 156, with the variations in the pattern explained below. See page 168 for the bonnet.

Sizes
3 (6) 9 (12) 24 months

Measurements
Full length: approx. 65 (70) 75 (80) 80cm (including flounce)

Yarn
Permin Elise, 90% cotton and 10% cashmere, 115 metres/25g
Gepard Linen Unika, 100% extra-fine linen, 160 metres/50g
Colour A: Permin Elise: 881109 raw white
Colour B: Gepard Linen Unika: 100 white
Quantity: 150 (175) 200 (225) 250g colour A, 100 (150) 150 (150) 200g colour B

Other materials
1 mother-of-pearl button: approx. 1.5cm in diameter
Foil tape or satin ribbon for the yoke

Crochet hooks
3mm and 3.5mm

Tension
28 htr BLO x 18 rounds = 10 x 10cm
23 dc x 28 rounds in pattern = 10 x 10cm

Note
Work according to pattern for Amanda's dress on p. 156 with the yarn types mentioned above and otherwise with the variations described in this section.

Work the yoke in colour A.

The bottom in pattern is worked with both the yarns, colours A and B.

Be sure to switch to a 3.5mm hook when you come to the skirt pattern.

Thread a length of elastic or satin ribbon through the dress just below the yoke, passing the elastic or ribbon in and out between stitches at 4–5 stitch intervals.

CHRISTENING DRESS

Start with a 3mm hook. Change to 3.5mm hook on the pattern. Work according to pattern for Amanda's dress on p. 156 until gown measures 60 (65) 70 (75) 75cm – 5cm before full length of gown.

Then work a peplum with a 3mm hook as described in the pattern for Milla's or Julie's top on pp. 47 and 106. Work 7 (7) 7 (9) 9 rounds in total on flounce.

Work long sleeves with 3mm hook as described for Amanda's dress.

Lulu's bonnet

The bonnet is crocheted with a round neck piece in half treble crochet rib with patterned crochet on the sides. The pattern matches Leo's christening gown.

Sizes
3 (6) 9 (12) 18 months

Measurements
The neck piece is 10 (11) 11 (12) 12cm in diameter
The sides measure 9 (10.5) 12 (13) 14cm

Yarn
Permin Elise, 90% cotton and 10% cashmere, 115meters/25g
Gepard Linen Unika, 100% extra-fine linen, 160 metres/50g
Colour A: Permin Elise 881109 raw white
Colour B: Gepard Linen Unika 100 white
Quantity: 25g colour A, 50g colour B (applies to all sizes)

Crochet hooks
3mm and 3.5mm

Tension
28 htr BLO x 18 rounds = 10 x 10cm

Note
Make sure you work the very last st on a row; it can be hard to find when working BLO.
Turning chains do not count towards the total stitch count.
The round neck piece is worked with htr BLO from round 2, unless otherwise stated in pattern.
The pattern is worked through both loops and not BLO.
See p. 19 for how to work spike stitches.

When changing colour, pull the new colour yarn through at the last pull-through on the last st of the old colour. Make sure that the yarn not in use is brought up to the WS of the piece.

Decorative pattern: divisible by 4 + 3 sts

Row 1 (RS): change to colour B. Ch 1, dc 1 in next 3 sts, *ch 2, skip 1 st, dc 1 in next 3 sts*, rep from * to * to end. Turn piece.

Row 2: ch 1, dc 1 in first 3 sts, *ch 2, skip ch-space, dc 1 in next 3 sts*, rep from * to * to end. Turn.

Row 3: Change to colour A. Ch 1, *dc 1, ch 2, skip 1 st, dc 1 in next st, then work 1 spike stitch as follows: 1 tr around 2-ch space and straight down in st 3 rows below*, rep from * to * to end. Finish with 1 dc, 2 ch, skip 1 st, 1 dc. Turn.

Row 4: Ch 1, 1 dc, *ch 2, skip ch-space, dc 1 in next 3 sts*, rep from * to * to end. Finish with 2 ch, skip ch-space, 1 dc. Turn.

Row 5: Change to colour B. Ch 1, *dc 1 in next st, then work 1 spike stitch as follows: 1 tr around 2-ch space and straight down in st 3 rows below; 1 dc, 2 ch, skip 1 st*, rep from * to * to end. Omit last 2 ch on last repeat. Turn.

Row 6: ch 1, dc 1 in first 3 sts *ch 2, skip ch-space, dc 1 in next 3 sts*, rep from * to * to end. Turn.

Rep rows 3–6, to measurements given in pattern below or to desired length.
Finish pattern with the following 2 rows:

Row 7: Change to colour A. Ch 1, *1 dc in next 3 sts, then 1 spike stitch as follows: 1 tr around 2-ch space and straight down in sts 3 rows below*, rep from * to * to end, ending with 1 dc in last 3 sts.

Row 8: ch 1, dc 1 in each st.

NECK

Start with colour A and 3mm hook.

Round 1 (RS): make a magic loop with 9 htr. Close round with 1 sl st in 1st htr (9 sts). Turn and work the other way around.

Round 2: Ch 2, 2 htr BLO in every st. Close round with 1 sl st in 1st htr (18 sts). Turn.

Round 3: ch 2, work htr in BLO and inc 1 in every 2nd st. Close round with 1 sl st in 1st htr (27 sts). Turn.

Round 4: Ch 2, work htr in BLO and inc 1 in every 3rd st. Close round with 1 sl st in 1st htr (36 sts). Turn.

Continue as follows with htr rib with 9 incs on each round:
On round 5, inc every 4th st, on 6th round, inc every 5th st and so on.
Make sure to distribute the incs evenly (and not over the top of each other from round to round). The neck piece should be circular and not square. Rep round with increases until you have worked a total of 9 (10) 10 (11) 11 rounds (81 (90) 90 (99) 99 sts).

Next round (RS): ch 1, sl st 1 for the next 8 (9) rounds. 10 (10) 10 sts, ch 1, dc 1 in the next 63 (72) 70 (79) 79 sts, 1 sl st in the last 8 (9) 10 (10) 10 sts.

Break yarn and fasten off.

SIDES

Now work back and forth over 63 (72) 70 (79) 79 sts in dc rib and pattern. Sl st is at the bottom of hat and these sts should not be worked.

Row 1 (RS): change to 3.5 mm hook. Ch 1, dc 1 in same st, dc 1 BLO for next 4 (5) 5 (5) 6 sts (dc rib), change to colour B and start the decorative pattern by following the 1st row of the pattern. Work pattern (through both loops and no longer BLO) over the next 52 (59) 59 (67) 67 sts, at the same time work 1 dec in size 3 and 6 months, 1 dec in size 9 months and 2 dec in size 18 months (the number of stitches must be divisible by 4 + 3 sts). Change to colour A, 1 dc BLO in the last 5 (6) 6 (6) 7 sts (dc rib). Keep a small ball of Elise yarn on this side of hat to change to when working with colour B in pattern (62 (71) 71 (79) 81 sts in total). Turn.

Row 2: ch 1, 5 (6) 6 (6) 7 dc BLO, 52 (59) 59 (67) 67 sts in pattern, 5 (6) 6 (6) 7 dc BLO (62 (71) 71 (79) 81 sts in total). Turn.

Rep row 2 with pattern in middle stitches and dc rib in outermost edge stitches as described.

Work until pattern measures 6.5 (7) 8 (8.5) 9.5cm. Finish the pattern with rows 7–8.

EDGE

Continue working with colour A and 3mm hook; at front of hat work 5 (6) 6 (7) 7 rows with htr rib and continue dc rib at sides.

Finish with a firm edge with 1 sl st in every st through both loops (or crab stitch or picot).

At the same time as edge of sl sts work tie band in each side as follows: just after first htr rib work 50 (60) 60 (60) 60 ch, 1 htr in 2nd ch from hook, then 1 sl st in every ch. Then sl

sts in the bonnet edge itself, and finally a tie on the other side, similar to the first. Break yarn and fasten off.

FINISH

Weave in any remaining ends.
Gently steam and press the bonnet under a dry cloth.

Tip

Instead of a tie you can pull a loop through the bottom edge of the bonnet.

ACCESSORIES

Ashe's bib

This bib is worked in one piece, starting mid-front in a magic circle. Chain stitch and double crochet rib are used to create the shape. The bib is actually a half circle with straps. There is a button at the neck and the bobbles are crocheted as decoration. Krea Deluxe Organic Cotton is a great yarn to crochet with, as the thread is braided and cannot split while crocheting. Choose your own colour for the bib. The yarn is available in various beautiful colours and in 25g and 50g skeins.

Sizes
6 (18) months

Measurements
Height centre front: approx. 9 (10)cm

Yarn
Krea Deluxe Organic Cotton, 100% organic cotton, 165 metres/50g
Colours: 45 bottle green, 52 cognac, 07 powder pink, 22 light blue
Quantity: 20 (25)g

Other materials
1 button: 1.5–2cm in diameter

Crochet hook
3mm

Tension
28 dc BLO x 24 rows = 10 x 10cm

Note
Work dc back and forth in rows. Turn after every row.

Please count after you work the very last st on a row; it can be hard to find the last st when working BLO.

Work 1 ch for turning chain, whether working sl sts or dc. The turning chain does not count towards the total stitch count.

Pattern
All sl sts and dc are worked BLO from row 2 unless otherwise stated in the pattern.

Bobbles
Work 4 incomplete tr in one st (omit last pull-through in each tr) – there are then 5 loops on hook. Wrap yarn around hook and pull through 5 loops at once.
Loops should be relatively loose and of equal length on the thick part of hook: pull loops down and straighten with left hand. This will help the yarn slip through 5 loops more easily. As a plus, it makes a nice big bobble. Tighten so the bobble gathers and appears on the opposite side of the piece (that is, on the RS of the bib), 1 dc in the next st. Dc should also be tightened as it forces the bobble to arc. Work alternately 1 bobble stitch and 1 dc.

BIB

With the selected colour:
Row 1 (RS): make a magic ring with 7 dc.
Close round with 1 sl st in 1st st. This is the
base mid-front of the bib (7 sts).

Place a sl st on RS if desired.

Row 2 (RS again): 1 sl st in first 3 sts (not to
be worked further), ch 1, 2 dc (inc) in each of
next 4 sts BLO (8 sts). Turn.

Row 3: ch 1, *1 dc, inc 1*, rep from * to *
row (12 sts). Turn.

Row 4: ch 1, *2 dc, inc 1*, rep from * to *
(16 sts). Turn.

Rep row with incs 8 (10) more times with one
extra st between incs from row to row: 3 dc
between incs on 5th row, 4 dc between on 6th
row and so on. Distribute 4 incs evenly on
every row and not on top of each other from
row to row. The half circle should be round
and not square (48 (56) sts). Work 25 (27) ch
for loop to extend 12th (14th) row (total 73
(83) sts).

Row 13 (15): 1 sl st in 2nd ch from hook, 1 sl
st in next 7 (8) ch, 1 dc in each of last ch.
Work dc in sts of half circle, at the same time
work 4 incs evenly spaced (76 (86) sts). Work
25 (27) ch for extension of 13th (15th) row
(101 (113) sts in total). Turn.

Row 14 (16): 1 sl st in 2nd ch from hook, 1
sl st in next 7 (8) ch, 1 dc in each of last ch.
Work dc in next sts on piece and work at the
same time 6 incs evenly spaced; for the last 8
(9) sts, work 1 sl st BLO (total 106 (118) sts).
Turn.

Do not work incs on the part of the strap
where you work sl sts.

Row 15 (17): ch 1, sl st 1 in each of the next 8

(9) sts, dc 1 in each of the next sts on piece, at
the same time work 6 incs evenly distributed
on semicircle and straps; for the last 8 (9) sts
work sl sts (112 (124) sts).

Row 16 (18): ch 1, sl st in next 8 (9) sts, dc 1
in each st to last 8 (9) sts, work 6 incs evenly
on semicircle and straps; sl st in last 8 (9) sts
(118 (130) sts). Turn.

Row 17 (19): work a buttonhole at the
beginning of this row as follows: ch 1, sl st in
first 3 sts, ch 3, skip 3 sts, sl st in next 2 sts,
(3) sts, 1 dc in each st for the last 8 (9) sts, at
the same time work 6 incs evenly distributed
on half circle and straps, 1 sl st in the last 8
(9) sts (124 (136) sts).

Row 18 (20): ch 1, sl st in next 8 (9) sts, dc 1
in every st until last 8 (9) sts, work
at the same time 6 incs evenly distributed on
semicircle and straps, 1 sl st in last 8 (9) sts,
of which sl sts must be worked in each of the
3 ch in buttonhole (130 (142) sts).

Row 19 (21): ch 1, sl st in next 8 (9) sts, dc 1,
then work bobble pattern through both loops
until last 8 (9) sts, when sl st is worked. Do
not work incs on this row. There are 58 (64)
bobbles in total (130 (142) sts).

Row 20 (22): ch 1, sl st each of the next 8 (9)
sts, dc through both loops 1 until the last 8

Tip

*Linen is a good yarn to use to make bibs
with as linen is absorbent and is very
hard-wearing. Linen can be a little stiff
and stringy to work with, but after
washing and tumble-drying it becomes
soft and pliable.*

(9) sts, at the same time work 6 incs evenly distributed on the half circle and straps, sl st the next 8 (9) sts (136 (148) sts).

Note: Where possible work incs on top of the large bobble stitches on row 20 (22).

Rep row 20 (22) 3 more times, but work sl sts and dc BLO again (154 (166) sts).

Round 24 (26): ch 1, sl st in first 8 (9) sts, sl st through both loops in next 34 (39) sts, dc 1 BLO until 42 (48) sts remain, in which work through both loops until last 8 (9) sts, sl st in BLO in each of last 8 (9) sts). Do not work incs on this row (154 (166) sts).

Note: one extra row is worked on the strap on one side of the bib.

Break yarn and fasten off.

Work sl sts, at edge of bib from RS, where bobbles are visible. Work sl st from left to right as follows: after 40 (46) sl sts, join yarn in 1st dc, through both loops, and work 1 sl st in each dc to beg of sl sts. If preferred, choose a border with crab or picot stitches. Break yarn and finish off.

FINISHING
Weave in any remaining ends and sew a button on one strap.
Steam and press the bib under a dry cloth without flattening the bobbles.

Tip

Use leftover bamboo and mercerised cotton yarn to make some bibs.

Georg's cap & mittens

This is a well-fitting cap and matching mittens. It is based on the classic Danish devil cap shape, but is more helmet-like and round at the top. The cap is worked in one piece from the top down. The tie is worked at the same time as the finishing edge. The increases and decreases create the shape of the cap. The pattern is half treble crochet rib, which gives elasticity and a ribbed look.

Sizes
Hat: 0 (3) 6 (9) 12 (24) months
Mittens: 0 (3) 6 (9) 12 months
The mittens are best suited for the very young, therefore the largest size is 12 months.

Measurements
Hat: Fits a head circumference of approx. 36 (40) 46 (48) 50 (52)cm
Mittens: circumference 13 (13) 16 (16)cm, length 8 (9) 10 (11) 11cm

Yarn
Gepard CottonWool 3 Organic, 50% cotton and 50% wool, 230 metres/50g
Quantity: 50 (100) 100 (100) 100 (100)g for the whole set

Other materials
Length of elastic for mittens: approx. 50cm

Crochet hook
3mm

Tension
28 htr BLO x 18 rounds = 10 x 10cm

Note
Turn piece every round so that you can work in the opposite direction.

Start each round with 2 ch and finish each round with 1 sl st in 1st htr through both loops. This is not mentioned in the pattern.

Turning chains are not counted in the total stitch count.

Make sure that increases are evenly distributed from round to round at the beginning so that the piece is circular. If the incs are worked on top of each other, the piece will be jagged at the edges.

The join from round to round will be even when you close the rounds with slip stitch into the first stitch. See the technique on p. 18.

It is important to keep track of the stitch count.

Pattern
Work BLO from round 2 unless otherwise stated in pattern.

HAT

Start with a magic ring:

Round 1 (RS): ch 2, 9 htr into the magic ring. Close round with 1 sl st in 1st htr (9 htr). Turn and work the other way around.

If you like, put a stitch marker on RS so that you always know where you are on the piece.

Increase on each of the following rounds with 9 htr. That is 9 incs. Work 1 htr in each st between incs. Depending on the size of the hat, the first incs stop after 8 (9) 10 (10) 11 (11) rounds. Then go to the size in the pattern that you are going to work.

Round 2 (WS): 2 htr in every htr, turn piece every round (18 htr).
Round 3: 2 htr in every 2nd htr (27 htr).
Round 4: 2 htr in every 3rd htr (36 htr).
Round 5: 2 htr in every 4th htr (45 htr).
Round 6: 2 htr in every 5th htr (54 htr).
Round 7: 2 htr in every 6th htr (63 htr).
Round 8: 2 htr in every 7th htr (72 htr) – cont from here to size 0 months.
Round 9: 2 htr in every 8th htr (81 htr) – cont from here to size 3 months.
Round 10: 2 htr in every 9th htr (90 htr) – cont from here to size 6 or 9 months.
Round 11: 2 htr in every 10th htr (99 htr) – cont from here to size 12 or 24 months.

0 MONTHS

Round 9: 2 htr in every 12 htr (78 sts).
Round 10: 1 htr in every htr in the round (78 sts).
Round 11: 2 htr in every 13 htr (84 sts).
Round 12: 1 htr in every htr in the round (84 sts).
Now work the sides of the hat.
Round 13: From RS, work 1 inc, 13 htr, fan inc (see p. 19) in each of the next 2 htr, 13 htr, 2 inc, 7 htr, fan inc in the next 2 htr, 7 htr, 2 inc, 13 htr, fan inc in the next 2 htr, 2 htr, 13

Tip

Add a faux fur pompom to the hat, or a pompom made of yarn.

htr and 1 dec (90 sts).
Round 14: 1 dec, 30 htr, 2 dec, 18 htr, 2 dec, 30 htr, 1 dec (84 sts).
Rep rounds 13 and 14 5 more times. There should be a total of 24 rounds. Go to Edge and work from RS.

3 MONTHS

Round 10: 1 htr in each htr in the round (81 sts).
Round 11: Work 7 incs evenly on this round (88 sts).
Round 12: 1 htr in every htr in the round (88 sts).
Round 13: Work 8 incs evenly distributed on this round (96 sts).
Round 14: 1 htr in every htr in the round (96 sts).
Now work the sides of the hat.
Round 15: From RS work 1 dec, 15 htr, fan inc in each of the next 2 htr, 15 htr, 2 dec, 9 htr, fan inc in each of the next 2 htr, 9 htr, 2 dec, 15 htr, fan inc in each of the next 2 htr, 15 htr, 1 dec (102 sts).
Round 16: 1 dec, 34 htr, 2 dec, 22 htr, 2 dec, 34 htr and 1 dec (96 sts).
Rep rounds 15 and 16 5 more times. There should be 26 rounds in total. Go to Edge and work from RS.

6 MONTHS

Round 11: 1 htr in every htr in the round (90 sts).
Round 12: Work 9 incs evenly on round (99 sts).

Round 13: 1 htr in every htr in the round (99 sts).
Round 14: Work 9 incs evenly on round (108 sts).
Round 15: 1 htr in every htr in the round (108 sts).
Round 16: Work 6 incs evenly on round (114 sts).
Now work the sides of the hat.
Round 17: From RS, work 1 dec, 19 htr, fan inc in each of the next 2 htr, 19 htr, 2 dec, 10 htr, fan inc in each of the next 2 htr, 2 htr, 10 htr, 2 dec, 19 htr, fan inc in each of the next 2 htr, 19 htr, 1 dec (120 sts).
Round 18: 1 dec, 42 htr, 2 dec, 24 htr, 2 dec, 42 htr, 1 dec (114 sts).
Rep rounds 17 and 18 5 more times and finish with another round 17. There should be 29 rounds in total. Go to Edge and work from RS.

9 MONTHS

Round 11: 1 htr in every htr in the round (90 sts).
Round 12: Work 9 incs evenly on round (99 sts).
Round 13: 1 htr in every htr in the round (99 sts).
Round 14: Work 9 incs evenly on round (108 sts).
Round 15: 1 htr in every htr in the round (108 sts).
Round 16: Work 12 incs evenly on round (120 sts).
Now work the sides of the hat.
Round 17: From RS, work 1 inc, 20 htr, fan inc in each of the next 2 htr, 20 htr, 2 dec, 12 htr, fan inc in each of the next 2 htr, 2 htr, 12 htr, 2 dec, 20 htr, fan inc in each of the next 2 htr, 20 htr, 1 dec (126 hdc).
Round 18: 1 dec, 44 htr, 2 dec, 28 htr, 2 dec, 44 htr, 1 dec (120 sts).
Rep round 17 and 18 7 more times. Do not work round 18 the last time.

There should be 31 rounds in total. Go to Edge and work from RS.

12 MONTHS

Round 12: 1 htr in every htr in the round (99 sts).
Round 13: Work 9 htr evenly on round (108 sts).
Round 14: 1 htr in every htr in the round (108 sts).
Round 15: Work 9 incs evenly on round (117 sts).
Round 16: 1 htr in every htr in the round (117 sts).
Round 17: Work 9 incs evenly on round (126 sts).
Round 18: 1 htr in every htr in the round (126 sts).
Now work the sides of the hat.
Round 19: From RS, work 1 dec, 21 htr, fan inc in each of the next 2 htr, 21 htr, 2 dec, 12 htr, fan inc in each of the next 2 htr, 2 htr, 12 htr, 2 dec, 21 htr, fan inc in each of the next 2 htr, 21 htr, 1 dec (132 sts).
Round 20: 1 dec, 46 htr, 2 dec, 28 htr, 2 dec, 46 htr, 1 dec (126 sts).

Rep rounds 19 and 20 6 more times. There should be 32 rounds in total. Go to Edge and work from RS.

24 MONTHS
Work up to 18th round on size 12 months.
Round 19: Work 6 incs evenly on round (132 sts).
Round 20: 1 htr in every htr around (132 sts).
Now work the sides of the hat.
Round 21: From RS, work 1 dec, 22 htr, fan inc in each of the next 2 htr, 22 htr, 2 dec, 13 htr, fan inc in each of the next 2 htr, 2 htr, 13 htr, 2 dec, 22 htr, fan inc in each of the next 2 htr, 22 htr, 1 dec (138 sts).
Round 22: 1 dec, 48 htr, 2 dec, 30 htr, 2 dec, 48 htr, 1 dec (132 sts).
Rep rounds 21 and 22 6 more times. Do not work round 22 the last time. There should be 33 rounds in total. Go to Edge and work from RS.

EDGE
Without breaking yarn, work edge and tie from RS as follows:
Start with 1 ch. Choose the edge you want: slip stitch, picot stitch or crab stitch.

Slip stitch: 1 sl st in every htr through both loops.
Picot stitch: *1 dc in next st, ch 3, 1 dc in 3rd ch from hook, skip 1 or 2 sts*, rep from * to * around.
Crab stitch: 1 dc from left to right in every htr (i.e. work dc the opposite way to usual).

At the same time as the edge, work two ties on each side of beg of round, at and between the two fan shapes: Work 50 (55) 55 (60) 60 (60) ch. Work 1 htr in 2nd ch from hook, 1 sl st in every ch back to cap edge.
Break yarn and fasten off.

MITTENS
Work as described in pattern for cap until there are 36 (36) 45 (45) 45 htr on a round. Then work straight with htr rib until piece measures 8 (9) 10 (11) 11cm.
Finish piece with the edge you want. Work edge from RS as described in hat pattern.
Break yarn and fasten off.
Repeat for second mitten.

FINISHING
Weave in any remaining ends of hat and mittens.
There are only two ends to fasten on each piece. Insert a length of elastic in the wrist by passing it in and out between htr sts on 3rd round from edge at 4-st intervals, then tie a knot.
Gently steam and press hat and mittens under a dry cloth.

Tip

Gepard My Fine Wool is a very fine yarn alternative for hats and mittens, being an elastic and soft yarn for baby. If you want a longer cuff on the mitten, you can work 6–8 rounds more rib. Then insert the elastic in round 8–10 from the edge.

Manna's moccasins

Manna's moccasins are crocheted in one piece starting on an oval sole. The sole is worked with half treble crochet, while the top of the shoe is worked with half treble crochet rib. On the top of the shoe work back and forth in the round, closing and joining at heel. With the addition of elastic, the shoes will stay on the baby's foot and are not very easy to kick off.

Sizes
0 (3) 6 months

Measurements
Width of sole: approx. 6cm incl. edge (all sizes)
Length of sole: approx. 10 (11) 12cm
Height: approx. 8 (9) 10cm

Yarn
Önling No 2, 100% superfine merino, 120 metres/25g

Colour:
73 raw white, 7839 marzipan, 40127 olive yellow, 3622 very light grey or 3559 light grey

Other materials
Length of elastic: 50–60cm

Crochet hook
3.5mm

Tension
22 htr x 15 rows = 10 x 10cm

Note
Place a stitch marker at the RS of the heel so that you are always aware of where you are on the piece.
Turning chains do not count in the total number of stitches.

Pattern
Work BLO on top of shoe unless otherwise stated in pattern. The sole stitches are worked plain, through both loops.

SOLE

Work 12 (14) 16 ch in your choice of yarn colour.

Round 1 (RS): 2 htr in 3rd ch from hook, 1 htr in every ch until penultimate ch, 5 htr in last ch (toe). Work 1 htr in every st on underside of ch until last st. (Here you can take the yarn end with you and work around it on round 1. This is a good way to fasten yarn ends.), 3 htr in last st (heel). Finish round with 1 sl st in 1st st on round (26 (30) 34 sts).

Round 2 (RS): ch 2, 2 htr in each of the next 2 sts, 1 htr in each st to the 5 sts in the toe, 2 htr in each of the 5 sts in the toe, 1 htr in each st on the underside to the last 3 sts, 2 htr in each of the last 3 sts.

Round 3 (RS): ch 2, htr 2 in 1st st, htr 1 in next st, htr 2 in 3rd st on round. Continue with 1 htr in each htr along the side to toe. Make 5 incs with 1 htr between incs. Follow round, working 1 htr in every st on underside, and work 3 htr in every other st to end of round (before heel), closing round with 1 sl st in 1st htr (46 (50) 54 sts).

Round 4 (RS): ch 2, htr 1 in 1st st, htr 2 in next st, 1 htr in each of next 2 sts, 2 htr in next st (5th st). Continue with 1 htr in every st on the side until toe, where you work 5 incs with 2 htr between each inc. Continue the round, work 1 htr in every st on underside, and finish with 3 htr in every 3rd st (before heel), close round with 1 sl st in 1st htr (56 (60) 64 sts).

Edge sole with 1 sl st in every htr (56 (60) 64 sts).
Sole is finished, but do not break yarn. Continue to the top of the shoe.

TOP

On sides/top of shoe, work htr rib (unless otherwise indicated). To achieve a ribbed pattern, turn and work in the opposite direction for each new round. Make sure to start mid-back of heel and let the join from round to round go up in a straight line. You can take the stitch marker up along heel on RS (see p. 18). Work in the very first st after turning stitches.

Round 1 (RS): Work 1 sl st BLO mid-back of heel and work 2 ch. Work 1st htr where yarn is attached with 2 ch, then 1 htr in every st all the way around 4th round of sole (stitch chains behind sl st round). Close round with 1 sl st in 1st htr through both loops. Turn and work the opposite way around (56 (60) 64 sts).

Close and turn in the same way on the remaining rounds.

Round 2 (WS): ch 2, 1 htr in each htr in the round. Close round with 1 sl st in 1st htr (56 (60) 64 sts). Turn.

Round 3 (RS): ch 2, 1 htr in first 19 (20) 21 sts to front 18 (20) 22 sts on toe, work 9 (10) 11 decs. Continue with 1 htr in each of the last 19 (20) 21 sts on round. Close round with 1 sl st in 1st htr. (47 (50) 53 sts). Turn.

Round 4: ch 2, 1 htr in every htr in the round. Close round with 1 sl st in 1st htr. (47 (50) 53 sts). Turn.

Tip

Work an edge with e.g. picot stitches or chain stitches at the top of shoe (see page 183).

Tip

*This would be a great project to use up
your leftover yarn.*

Round 5: Ch 2, 1 htr in each of the 16 (17)
17 sts to the front 14 (16) 18 sts on toe, work
7 (8) 9 decs along toe. Continue with 1 htr
in the next 17 (17) 18 sts on round and close
round with 1 sl st in 1st htr. (40 (42) 44 sts).
Turn.

Round 6: Ch 2, 1 htr in every st in the round.
Close with 1 sl st in 1st htr. (40 (42) 44 sts).
Turn.

Round 7: Ch 2, 1 htr in each of the 17 (18)
19 sts to the front 6 (6) 6 sts on toe, work
decs 3 (3) 3 times along toe. Continue with 1
htr in the next 17 (18) 19 sts on round, and

close round with 1 sl st in 1st htr. (37 (39) 41
sts). Turn.

Work 5 (6) 7 rounds straight (or to desired
height) in htr rib, changing crochet direction
each round.

To finish, work an edge from RS with 1 sl st
in each htr through both loops. Make sure
to work sl sts loosely as the edge should be
able to give. Use a larger hook for sl sts if
necessary.
Break yarn and finish off, then work a second
shoe the same.

FINISHING

Weave in any remaining ends.
Pull a length of elastic between stitches on
round 2 of Top after last dec of toe.

Peer Bo's sunhat

This summer hat brings its own shade in the form of the ruffled brim. It's soft, floppy and comfortable for a baby to wear. It is worked in one piece from the top down. Work double crochet in the round in a spiral, then work a two-colour pattern border. The brim is half treble. Anni's T-shirt matches in yarn and colours (see p. 122).

Sizes
0 (4) 9 (12) 24 months

Measurements
Fits a head circumference of approximately
36 (40) 46 (48) 52cm

Yarn
Sandnes Tynn Line, 53% cotton, 33% viscose
and 14% linen, 220 metres/50g
Colour A: chalky 1015
Colour B: terracotta 3513
Quantity: 50g of each colour (for to all sizes)

Crochet hook
3mm

Tension
28 dc x 34 rounds = 10 x 10cm

Note
The join in the patterned border and on the brim will be straight when you close the round with sl st in the first st (see p. 18).

See p. 19 for how to work spike stitches.

When changing colour, pull the new colour of yarn through at the start of the round. Only then work a turn stitch (as shown in pattern) with the new colour. Make sure that the yarn not in use is brought up to the WS of the piece.

Two-colour pattern: divisible by 4 sts
Round 1 (RS): change to colour B. Ch 1, dc 1 in next 3 sts, *ch 2, skip 1 st, dc 1 in next 3 sts*, rep from * to * around. Finish round with 2 ch, skip 1 st, 1 sl st in 1st dc. Turn piece and work the opposite way.

Round 2: ch 1, dc 1 in 1st st, ch 2, skip ch-space, dc 1 in next 3 sts*, rep from * to * to end. Finish round with 2 ch, skip ch-space, and work 1 dc in each of the last 2 sts. Turn.

Round 3: Change to colour A. Ch 1, *ch 1, dc 2, skip 1 st, ch 1 in next st, then work 1

spike stitch as follows: 1 tr around 2-ch space and straight down in st 3 rows below*, rep from * to * to end. Finish with 1 sl st in 1st dc. Turn.

Round 4: Ch 1, 3 dc, *ch 2, skip ch-space, dc 1 in next 3 sts*, rep from * to * to end. Finish with 2 ch, skip ch-space, and close round with 1 sl st in 1st dc. Turn.

Round 5: Change to color B. Ch 1, *1 dc in (first) next st, then work 1 spike stitch as follows: 1 tr around 2-ch space and straight down in st 3 rows below; ch 1, 2 ch, skip 1 st*, rep from * to * to end. Finish round with 1 sl st in 1st dc. Turn.

Round 6: Ch 1, dc 1 in 1st st, *ch 2, skip ch-space, dc 1 in next 3 sts*, rep from * to * around. Finish with 2 ch, skip 2-ch space, 1 dc in the last 2 sts, and close round with 1 sl st in 1st dc. Turn.

Rep rows 3–6 to measurements given in pattern below or to desired length.

Finish pattern with the following 2 rounds:

Round 7 (RS): change to colour A. * 1 dc in first 3 sts, then 1 spike stitch as follows: 1 tr around 2-ch space and straight down in idle st 3 rounds below*, rep from * to * to end, ending with 1 dc in last 3 sts.

Round 8 (RS): 1 dc in every st round.

HAT

Round 1: Start with a magic circle and 6 dc in colour A.

Work dc in the round in a spiral with 6 incs on every round. When working in spiral rounds, do not close round with 1 sl st – there are no turning stitches and thus no visible transitions. Mark the beginning of a new round with a stitch marker. Let the stitch marker be carried forward from round to round.

Round 2: PM, 2 dc in every st (12 sts).
Round 3: 2 dc in every 2nd st (1 dc in the other sts) (18 sts).
Round 4: 2 dc in every 3rd st (1 dc in the other sts) (24 sts).
Round 5: 2 dc in every 4th st (1 dc in the other sts) (30 sts).

Inc 6 dc on every round so that there is one extra st between inc for every round.
Make sure that the incs are evenly distributed around the round so that the piece is circular: the incs should not lie evenly on top of each other from round to round, otherwise the piece will end up hexagonal.

Round 6: 2 dc in every 5th st (1 dc in the other sts) (36 sts).
Round 7: 2 dc in every 6th st (1 dc in the other sts) (42 sts).
Round 8: 1 dc in every st (42 sts).
Round 9: 2 dc in every 7th st (1 dc in the other sts) (48 sts).
Round 10: 2 dc in every 8th st (1 dc in the other sts) (54 sts).
Round 11: 2 dc in every 9th st (1 dc in the other sts) (60 sts).
Round 12: 1 dc in every st (60 sts).
Round 13: 2 dc in every 10th st (1 dc in the other sts) (66 sts).
Round 14: 2 dc in every 11th st (1 dc in the other sts) (72 sts).
Round 15: 2 dc in every 12th st (1 dc in the other sts) (78 sts).
Round 16: 1 dc in every st (78 sts).

Tip

Size 0 months could also be used as a doll's outfit.

Now go to the respective sizes.

0 MONTHS

Round 17: 2 dc in every 13th st (1 dc in the other sts) (84 sts).
Round 18: 1 dc in every st (84 sts).
Round 19: 2 dc in every 21st st (1 dc in the other sts) (88 sts).
Round 20: 1 dc in every st (88 sts).
Round 21: 2 dc in every 22nd st (1 dc in the other sts) (92 sts).

Go to "all sizes".

4 MONTHS

Round 17: 2 dc in every 13th st (1 dc in the other sts) (84 sts).
Round 18: 2 dc in every 14 sts (1 dc in the other sts) (90 sts).
Round 19: 1 dc in every st (90 sts).
Round 20: 2 dc in every 18th st (1 dc in the other sts) (95 sts).
Round 21: 1 dc in every st (95 sts).
Round 22: 2 dc in every 19th st (1 dc in the other sts) (100 sts).

Go to All Sizes.

9 MONTHS

Round 17: 2 dc in every 13th st (1 dc in the other sts) (84 sts).
Round 18: 2 dc in every 14th st (1 dc in the other sts) (90 sts).
Round 19: 2 dc in every 15th st (1 dc in the other sts) (96 sts).

Round 20: 1 dc in every st (96 sts).
Round 21: 2 dc in every 16th st (1 dc in the other sts) (102 sts).
Round 22: 2 dc in every 17th st (1 dc in the other sts) (108 sts).
Round 23: 1 dc in every st (108 sts).
Round 24: 2 dc in every 27th st (1 dc in the other sts) (112 sts).

Go to All Sizes.

12 MONTHS

Round 17: 2 dc in every 13th st (1 dc in the other sts) (84 sts).
Round 18: 2 dc in every 14th st (1 dc in the other sts) (90 sts).
Round 19: 2 dc in every 15th st (1 dc in the other sts) (96 sts).
Round 20: 1 dc in every st (96 sts).
Round 21: 2 dc in every 16th st (1 dc in the other sts) (102 sts).
Round 22: 2 dc in every 17th st (1 dc in the other sts) (108 sts).
Round 23: 1 dc in every st (108 sts).
Round 24: 2 dc in every 27th st (1 dc in the other sts) (112 sts).
Round 25: 2 dc in every 28th st (1 dc in the other sts) (116 sts).

Go to All Sizes.

24 MONTHS

Round 17: 2 dc in every 13th st (1 dc in the other sts) (84 sts).
Round 18: 2 dc in every 14th st (1 dc in the other sts) (90 sts).
Round 19: 2 dc in every 15th st (1 dc in the other sts) (96 sts).
Round 20: 1 dc in every st (96 sts).
Round 21: 2 dc in every 16th st (1 dc in the other sts) (102 sts).
Round 22: 2 dc in every 17th st (1 dc in the other sts) (108 sts).
Round 23: 2 dc in every 18th st (1 dc in the other sts) (114 sts).

Tip

The yarn has no elasticity, so you can pull a soft, transparent jewellery elastic through the piece just above the ruffle for a better fit.

Work from RS one round with 1 sl st in every st through both loops (or choose another edging – see p. 31).
Break yarn, finish off and fasten ends.

FINISHING
Weave in any remaining ends.
Steam and press the hat under a dry cloth.

Round 24: 1 dc in every st (114 sts).
Round 25: 1 dc in every st (114 sts).
Round 26: 2 dc in every 23rd st (1 dc in the other sts) (119 sts).
Round 27: 2 dc in every 24th st (1 dc in the other sts) (124 sts).

Go to All Sizes.

ALL SIZES
Work 6 (7) 9 (10) 10 rounds evenly with dc.
Close the last round with 1 sl st in last st.
Continue to let stitch marker follow up and start two-colour pattern: start with 1st round (RS).
When pattern piece measures approx. 4 (5) 6 (6) 7cm, finish with rounds 7–8 in pattern.
Go to Hat Brim.

HAT BRIM
Round 1 (RS): with colour A. Ch 2, htr 2 in every st in the round. Close round with 1 sl st. 1 htr through both loops now and on next rounds of brim. Turn and work the opposite way around (184 (200) 224 (232) 248 sts).

Round 2 (WS): 2 ch, 1 htr BLO in every st. Turn. (184 (200) 224 (232) 248 sts).

Round 3 (RS): ch 2, 1 htr in every st. Turn. (184 (200) 224 (232) 248 sts).
Rep rounds 2 and 3 until 5 (5) 5 (6) 6 rounds in total for brim.

Berthine's & Helene's collars

Krea Deluxe Organic Cotton is an easy and comfortable yarn to crochet with, as the thread is braided and cannot split while you are crocheting. The yarn is available in a multitude of beautiful colours and in 25g and 50g skeins. Berthine's collar is crocheted in half treble crochet and Helene's collar is crocheted in double crochet. Both designs work well as bibs. They can be tied at the neck or at the front. The collars are perfect as maternity gifts and a great little crochet project to have on the go.

Size
Berthine's collar: 6 (12) 18 months
Helene's collar: 6 (12) 18 months

Measurements
Neck width:
Berthine's collar: approx. 22 (24) 26cm
Helene's collar: approx. 21 (24) 26cm

Yarn
Krea Deluxe Organic Cotton, 100% organic cotton, 165 metres/50g
Colour:
Berthine's collar: 01 natural white, 40 light green, 22 light blue
Helene's collar: 16 pink, 45 bottle green
Quantity: 50g both models – all sizes

Crochet hook
3mm

Tension
28 dc BLO x 24 rows = 10 x 10cm
26 htr BLO x 20 rows = 10 x 10cm

Note
Make sure that you work the very last st on a row; it can be hard to find when working BLO.

Turning chains are not counted in the total stitch count.

Pattern
Both designs are worked BLO, starting from row 2, unless otherwise stated in pattern.

Tip

In many nurseries, ties are not allowed on clothing. It is possible to create a button closure instead. Do not work a tie, but only a row of sl sts along the neck edge and a long strap with 5 buttonholes at the end as follows: work 13 ch, 1 tr in 6th ch from hook, *1 ch, skip 1 st, 1 tr in next st*, rep from * to * a total of 3 times, finish with 1 ch and fasten the strand with a few sl sts in the side of collar. Sew on a button on the opposite side of collar.

BERTHINE'S COLLAR

Leave about 5 metres of yarn hanging at the beginning, as you will use this to work the tie and sl st edge in the neckline. Crochet a slip stitch edge and tie as soon as you can to avoid having to keep the yarn hanging during the rest of the work. See how at the end of the pattern.

Work 55 (61) 67 ch in chosen colour.
Row 1 (RS): 1 htr in 3rd ch from hook, 1 htr in next 4 sts, *fan inc (see p. 19) in next st, 1 htr in next 5 sts*, rep from * to * until no more sts remain. Inc a total of 8 (9) 10 times (69 (77) 85 sts in total). Turn.

If desired, insert a stitch marker on RS.

Row 2: ch 2, 1 htr (remember to work BLO from now on) in every st over (66 (77) 85 sts). Turn.

Row 3: ch 2, htr 1 in next 6 sts *fan inc, htr 1 in next 7 sts*, rep from * to * to end. Work 1

htr in last 6 sts (82 (95) 105 sts). Turn.
Rep rows 2 and 3 3 (4) 4 times. Inc 1 st at beg and end of row and 2 sts between fan inc from one odd-numbered row to next odd-numbered row. There are now a total of 9 (11) 11 rows on collar and 133 (167) 185 sts on row. There are 13 (15) 15 htr between fan incs.

Row 10 (12) 12 (WS): ch 1, sl st 1 in every st of row to through both loops.
A different edge finish can be chosen – see page 183.
Break yarn, finish off and fasten ends.

TIES AND EDGE FINISH

Take the 5m yarn end, work 50 (55) ch (work from where yarn is attached at the very bottom in extension of collar edge) and work 1 htr in 3rd ch from hook, 1 sl st in every ch (tie). Continue with 1 sl st in every st on RS of neckline. Continue with tie on opposite side as follows: work 50 (55) ch, then 1 htr in 3rd ch from hook, 1 sl st in every ch.
Break yarn, finish off and fasten end.

FINISHING

Steam and press the collar under a dry cloth.

HELEN'S COLLAR

Begin as described for Berthine's collar, allowing 5 metres of yarn for later use.

Work 60 (60) 66 ch in chosen colour.

Row 1 (RS): 1 dc in 2nd ch from hook, 1 dc in next 8 (8) 9 sts, *fan inc in next st, and 1 dc in next 9 (9) 10 sts*, rep from * to * to end. There are 5 (5) 5 incs on the row. Turn (69 (69) 75 sts).

Put a stitch marker on RS if you like.

Row 2: ch 1, dc 1 BLO in the first 10 (10) 11 sts, *ch 1, skip 1 st, dc 1 in the next 11 sts (11) 12 sts*, rep from * to * row, ending with 1 dc in the last 10 (10) 11 sts (69 (69) 75 sts) Turn.

Row 3: ch 1, dc 1 in all sts and work fan inc in ch-spaces (79 (79) 85 sts) Turn.

Row 4: ch 1, dc 1 in next 11 (11) 12 sts to middle st of fan, *ch 1, skip 1 st, 13 (13) 14 dc*, rep from * to * to end. Finish with 11 (11) 12 dc (79 (79) 85 sts) Turn.

Rep rows 3 and 4 5 (7) 8 times. Inc 1 st at beg and end of row and 2 sts between fan inc from one odd-numbered row to next odd-numbered row. There are a total of 129 (149) 165 sts with 23 (27) 28 sts between fan incs, and a total of 14 (18) 20 rows have been worked.

Row 15 (19) 21 (RS): ch 1, work an edge with picot stitches through both loops (see page 183). Work fan stitch in ch-loops. You can also choose a different edge finish such as sl st or crab stitch.

Break yarn, finish off, and fasten end.

Work neck edge and tie as described in pattern for Berthine's collar.

FINISHING
Gently steam and press the collar under a dry cloth.

BABY'S ROOM

Dagmar's elephant rattle

Play around with the colour choices for this cute elephant rattle. Three colours have been used for this design, but you could make a version in a single colour. Use a plastic rattle insert so the rattle can be machine washed.

Measurements
Height/width: approx. 10cm x 10cm

Yarn
Gepard Cotton Wool 3 Organic, 50% merino wool and 50% cotton, 230 metres/50g
Scraps in 591 aubergine, 803 forest green, 152 truffle

Other materials
Fibrefill (toy stuffing)
Flat plastic rattle insert
Wooden teething ring

Crochet hook
3mm

Tension
26 dc BLO x 24 rows = 10 x 10cm

Note
Make sure that you work the very last st on a row; it can be difficult to find when working BLO.
Turning chains are not counted in the total stitch count.

Pattern
All sts are worked BLO from row 2 unless otherwise stated in pattern.

Krea Deluxe Organic Cotton is perfect for the rattle. The yarn makes a slightly larger elephant than indicated in this pattern, about 11 x 11cm.

BODY 1

Leave a piece of yarn 30cm long for later use. Then work 22 ch with the chosen colour of yarn.

Row 1 (RS): 1 dc in 2nd ch from hook, 1 dc in every ch until last ch, 2 dc in last st. Turn with 1 ch (22 sts).
From here work dc BLO.
Row 2: 2 dc in 1st st, 1 dc in every st to end (23 sts). Turn.
Row 3: ch 1, dc 1 in each st until last st, dc 2 in last st (24 sts). Turn.
Row 4: ch 1, dc 2 in 1st st, dc 1 in every st (25 sts). Turn.
Row 5: ch 1, dc 1 in every st until last st, dc 2 in last st (26 sts). Turn.
Row 6: ch 1, dc 2 in 1st st, dc 1 in each st (27 sts). Turn.
Row 7: Repeat row 5 (28 sts).
Row 8: Repeat row 6 (29 sts).
Row 9: ch 1, dc 1 in every st (29 sts). Turn.
Row 10: ch 1, dc 1 in each of the first 22 sts. Turn.

Now work back leg of elephant (it is 9 rows wide).

Rows 11–13: Ch 1, dc 1 in each st of row (22 sts) Turn.
Row 14: ch 1, dc 1 in each st, ch 8, turn piece (29 sts).
Row 15: 1 dc in 2nd ch from hook, 1 dc in each ch and st. Turn (29 sts).
Rows 16–21: ch 1, dc 1 in each st (29 sts). Turn.

Now work front leg of elephant (7 rows wide).

Row 22 (elephant main round) ch 1, work dc 2 tog, 1 dc in each of the next 15 sts (16 sts). Turn.
Row 23: ch 1, dc 1 in each st. (16 sts).
Row 24: ch 1, dc 2 tog, dc 1 in each of the next sts (15 sts).
Continue by working 12 ch and turn piece.

Row 25: 1 dc in 2nd ch from hook, 1 dc in each st until last 2 sts, working dc 2 tog (25 sts). Turn.
Row 26: ch 1, dc 2 tog, dc 1 in each st in round (24 sts). Turn.
Row 27: ch 1, dc 1 in each st until the last 2 sts, dc 2 tog (23 sts). Turn.
Row 28: dc 2 tog, 1 dc in each st (22 sts). Break yarn.

TAIL

With long yarn end from beginning, work 14 ch, 1 htr in 2nd ch from hook, 1 sl st in remaining ch.
Finish off and fasten end.

EARS

In the chosen colour of yarn, work ear in a stitch line at the front of Body 1 in line with row 21 of front leg (see picture opposite).
Start on RS in 4th st from front leg and join yarn in loop with 1 ch.
Row 1: 1st dc in st where yarn is attached, 11 dc (12 sts). Turn.
Row 2: ch 1, dec 1, dc in every st until last st, inc 1 (12 sts). Turn.
Row 3: ch 1, htr 1 in 1st st, dc 1 in each st for last dc 2 together (12 sts).

Rep rows 2 and 3 until a total of 7 rows have been worked. Turn.
Row 8: ch 1, dec 2, dc 1 in each st until last st. Do not work last st (9 sts). Turn.
Row 9: ch 1, sl st in every st. Add an edging if desired with sl sts on edge of ear.
Break yarn, finish off and fasten ends.

BODY 2

Work one more body piece in desired colour yarn, but without yarn end for tail.
Do not break yarn after row 28, as you will need to continue yarn at finish and join of two body pieces.

Tip

Scraps of yarn suitable for a 3mm crochet hook are ideal for this rattle.

Work an ear on Body 2 after partially joining the two body pieces, so you can be sure that the ear is worked on the correct side of the body part. You work the ear from the same row as on Body 1: find a stitch on row 21 and start in 4th st from front leg.

STRAP FOR TEETHING RING

Crochet 11 ch with the chosen colour of yarn.
Row 1: 1 dc in 2nd ch from hook, 1 dc in every subsequent ch (10 sts). Turn.
Row 2: ch 1, dc 1 BLO in every st to end. (10 sts). Turn.

Work a total of 12 rows dc rib by repeating row 2. Break yarn, but wait to fasten ends until strap is crocheted onto elephant's back.

FINISHING

Work from RS on Body 1, but continue working with yarn from Body 2.
Place the parts on top of each other: trunk over trunk, legs over legs.
Work dc all the way around through both layers. On trunk and back legs, work 1 dc in every st (make sure to work dc evenly, as the edge is visible from RS all the way around the elephant. Find a system where you stick the crochet hook down through the two parts). Insert the toy stuffing and rattle insert along the way. Don't put in too much stuffing as the elephant should be fairly flat.

When the two parts are crocheted together, work an edge around the elephant with 1 sl st in every dc from RS, while attaching the strap to the back as follows: fold the strap around the teething ring, place it behind the dc edge, and work sl sts through dc on the elephant and simultaneously through the two layers of the strap.

Weave in all ends.
Sew a few extra stitches in the strap and ears with the yarn ends. This way, the ears will fit to the body and the strap with the teething ring will be extra secure on the elephant's back.

Holger's pacifier cord

The cord is worked in double crochet. This makes a quick baby gift and a fun little project to take on the go. Krea Deluxe Organic Cotton is a great yarn to crochet with, as the thread is braided and cannot split while you are crocheting. The yarn is available in a multitude of beautiful colours and also in smaller 25g skeins. Leftover yarns in linen, cotton, bamboo and blends of these types are also suitable.

Measurements
Length: max. 22cm
Width: approx. 2.5cm

Yarn
Krea Deluxe Organic Cotton, 100% organic cotton, 165 metres/50g
Quantity: Scrap (approx. 10g) of the chosen colour

Other materials
Clips of your choice

Crochet hook
3mm

Tension
28 dc BLO x 20 rows = 10 x 10cm

Note
Turning chains are not counted in the total number of stitches.

Pay attention when working in the round over a few sts: make sure to work the 1st dc in the very first loop after the turning chain. Then work 11 dc and close round, even though it looks as if there is one more loop to work.

Pattern
Work dc BLO from round 2 unless otherwise stated in pattern.

There is a hole in the cord which you will now close by working the 12 sts together as follows: work sts tog 2 by 2 with dc through both layers (6 sts).

Work 18 ch for loop in direct continuation of join without breaking yarn (see the green pacifier cord in the photo opposite). Fasten the chain with 1 sl st on the cord itself. Then work 1 sl st in every ch on loop and finally 1 sl st in the 6 dc.

Break the yarn and fasten off.

FINISHING

Use the yarn at the beginning to sew on a wooden clip or other clip.
Weave in all ends.

Tip

Depending on the chosen type of clip, you may have to sew the parts together or crochet a clip with 6 dc. If you use a silicone O-ring, do not crochet a loop at one end.

PACIFIER CORD

Round 1 (RS): beg with 6 dc in a magic ring and the chosen colour of yarn. Close round with 1 sl st in 1st dc and pull yarn end to tighten hole (6 sts).
Turn piece and work the other way round.

Round 2: ch 1, 2 htr in every st. Close round with sl st in 1st dc and turn (12 dc).

Round 3 (RS): ch 1, dc 1 in every st. Close round with 1 sl st in 1st dc through both loops, and turn (12 dc). Rep round 3 until piece measures 18cm.

Vidar's baby blanket

Crochet Vidar's baby blanket in organic superfine merino. The blanket is light and soft, neat on both sides and weighs only about 250g. Work half treble crochet and double crochet alternately on the different blocks. Find a colour combination that you like, or use the colour combination below, which features 12 different colours. The inspiration for the blanket comes from the patchwork pattern called 'log cabin'. Work 'block on block': start with block 1 and end with block 18. Follow the blocks and colours in the photo on page 210.

Measurements
Approx. 105 x 65cm

Yarn
Önling No 2, 100% superfine merino, 120 metres/25g
Colour A: pink 2947
Colour B: yellow 40127
Colour C: peach
Colour D: bottle green 0876
Colour E: beige 7839
Colour F: purple 095
Colour G: navy 3339
Colour H: light blue 3650
Colour I: petrol blue 2705
Colour J: light grey 3622
Colour K: charcoal grey 3563
Colour M: raw white 73
Quantity: 25g of A–J, 75g of K and 5g of M

Crochet hook
4mm

Tension
22–23 htr BLO x 14 rows = 10 x 10cm

22–23 dc BLO x 24 rows = 10 x 10cm
(measured without stretching the crochet)

Note
Please count after you work the very last st on a row; it can be hard to find when working BLO.

Turn with 2 ch when working htr and 1 ch when working dc – these turning chains are not counted in the total stitch count.

When changing colour, pull the new colour of yarn through the loop on the hook and work on the next block with the new colour of yarn.

When working the sides of a block, work 1 st per row of dc and 3 sts per 2 rows of htr.

Pick up stitches in the same way, row by row. Be consistent with the way you work the row ends to make the blanket even and equally neat on both sides.

Pattern
All sts are worked BLO from row 2 unless otherwise stated in pattern.

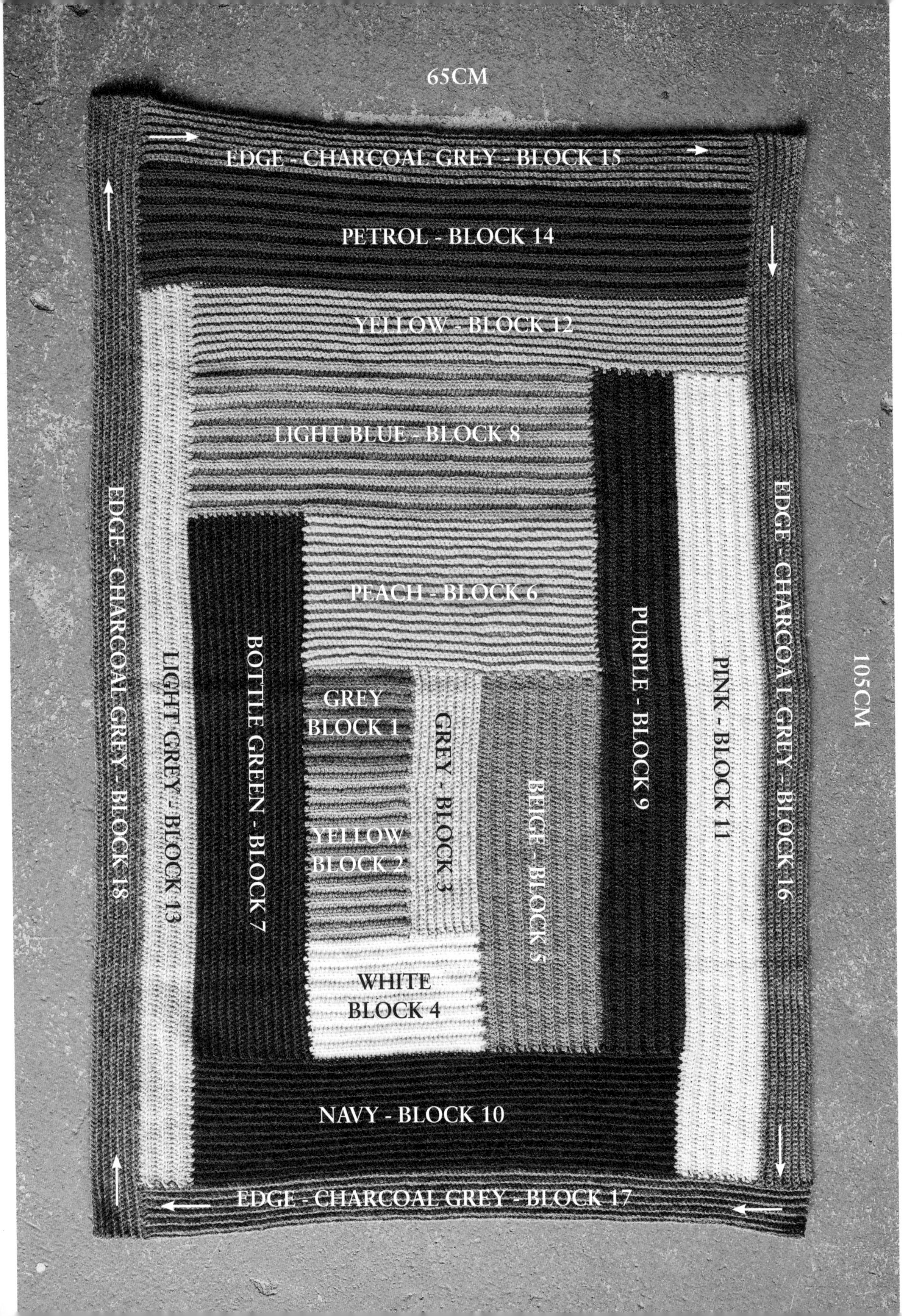

65CM

105CM

EDGE - CHARCOAL GREY - BLOCK 15

PETROL - BLOCK 14

YELLOW - BLOCK 12

LIGHT BLUE - BLOCK 8

PEACH - BLOCK 6

EDGE - CHARCOAL GREY - BLOCK 18

LIGHT GREY - BLOCK 13

BOTTLE GREEN - BLOCK 7

GREY BLOCK 1

YELLOW BLOCK 2

GREY - BLOCK 3

WHITE BLOCK 4

BEIGE - BLOCK 5

PURPLE - BLOCK 9

PINK - BLOCK 11

EDGE - CHARCOAL GREY - BLOCK 16

NAVY - BLOCK 10

EDGE - CHARCOAL GREY - BLOCK 17

BLANKET

Block 1
Work 25 ch with colour K (charcoal).
Row 1: 1 htr in 3rd ch from hook, 1 htr in every ch to end (23 sts). Turn.
Row 2: ch 2, 1 htr BLO in every st of row (23 sts). Turn.
Rep row 2 until a total of 12 rows have been worked with colour K.

Block 2
Change to colour B (yellow) and rep row 2 on block 1 until 23 rows have been worked in total with colour B.

Block 3
Change to colour J (light grey) and work 1 ch. Turn piece and work alongside blocks 1 and 2.
Row 1: work a total of 54 dc. Turn.
Row 2: ch 1, dc 1 (BLO) in every st of row (54 sts). Turn.
Rep row 2 until a total of 16 rows have been worked with colour J.

Block 4
Change to colour M (white) and work 2 ch. Turn piece and work htr along light grey and yellow blocks.
Row 1: work a total of 39 htr (BLO in yellow sts). Turn.
Row 2: Ch 2, 1 htr (BLO) in every st of row (39 sts). Turn.
Rep row 2 until a total of 16 rows (39 sts) have been worked with colour M.

Block 5
Change to colour E (beige) and work 2 ch. Turn piece and work alongside white and light grey blocks.
Row 1: Work a total of 78 htr (BLO in light grey sts). Turn.
Row 2: ch 2, 1 htr (BLO) in every st of row (78 sts). Turn.
Rep row 2 until a total of 17 rows have been worked with colour E.

Block 6
Change to colour C (peach) and work 1 ch. Turn piece and work dc along beige, light grey and charcoal grey blocks.

Row 1: work a total of 64 dc. Turn.
Row 2: ch 1, dc 1 (BLO) in every st of row (64 sts). Turn.
Rep row 2 until a total of 33 rows have been worked with colour C.

Block 7
Change to colour D (bottle green) and work 1 ch. Turn piece and work dc along peach, charcoal grey, yellow and white blocks.
Row 1: work a total of 109 dc. Turn.
Row 2: ch 1, dc 1 (BLO) in each st of row (109 sts). Turn.
Rep row 2 until a total of 26 rows have been worked with colour D.

Block 8
Change to colour H (light blue) and work 2 ch. Turn piece and work htr along bottle green and peach blocks.
Row 1: Work 88 htr (BLO) in total. Turn.
Row 2: ch 2, 1 htr (BLO) in every st of row (88 sts). Turn.
Rep row 2 until a total of 19 rows have been worked with colour H.

Block 9
Change to colour F (purple) and work 2 ch. Turn piece and work htr along light blue, peach and beige blocks.
Row 1: work a total of 141 htr (BLO in beige sts). Turn.
Row 2: ch 2, 1 htr (BLO) in every st of row (141 sts). Turn.
Rep row 2 until a total of 11 rows have been worked with colour F.

Block 10
Change to colour G (navy) and work 1 ch. Turn piece and work dc along purple, beige, white and green blocks.

Tip

The blanket is suitable for crocheting from various yarn scraps. Just observe the indicated tension if you want to achieve the same measurements. Rep row 2 until you have worked 28 rows in total with colour G.

Row 1: work a total of 106 dc (BLO in white sts). Turn.
Row 2: ch 1, dc 1 (BLO) in each st of row (106 sts). Turn.
Repeat the 2nd row until a total of 28 rows have been worked with color G.

Block 11

Change to colour A (pink) and work 2 ch. Turn piece and work htr along navy and purple blocks.
Row 1: work a total of 159 htr (BLO in purple sts). Turn.
Row 2: Ch 2, 1 htr (BLO) in every st of row (159 sts). Turn.
Rep row 2 until a total of 11 rows have been worked with colour A.

Block 12

Change to colour B (yellow) and work 1 ch. Turn piece and work dc along light pink, purple and light blue blocks.
Row 1: Work 121 dc in total (BLO in light blue sts). Turn.
Row 2: ch 1, dc 1 (BLO) in each st of row (121 sts). Turn.
Rep row 2 until a total of 17 rows have been worked with colour B.

Block 13

Change to colour J (light grey) and work 2 ch. Turn piece and work htr along yellow, light blue, green and navy blue blocks.

Row 1: Work a total of 181 htr (BLO in bottle green sts). Turn.
Row 2: Ch 2, 1 htr (BLO) in every st of row (181 sts). Turn.
Rep row 2 until a total of 7 rows have been worked with colour J.

Block 14

Change to colour I (petrol blue). Return to piece and join yarn with 2 ch in 1st st on side of block 13. Work htr over light grey and yellow blocks.
Row 1: work a total of 131 htr (BLO in yellow sts). Turn.
Row 2: Ch 2, 1 htr (BLO) in every st of row (131 sts). Turn.
Rep row 2 until a total of 15 rows have been worked with colour I.

BLANKET EDGE

Now work an edge with charcoal grey yarn. Work dc rib on all four sides of blanket; from block 15–18.

Block 15

Change to colour K (charcoal), ch 1, work dc along petrol blue coloured block.
Row 1: work a total of 131 dc BLO. Turn.
Row 2: ch 1, dc 1 (BLO) in every st of row (131 sts). Turn.
Rep row 2 until a total of 12 rows have been worked. Turn with 1 ch and finish block 15 with a row of 1 sl st in every st through both loops.

Block 16

Ch 1, turn piece and work dc along charcoal grey, petrol blue, yellow and pink blocks.
Row 1: work 209 dc in total (BLO in pink sts). Turn.
Row 2: ch 1, dc 1 (BLO) in each st of row (209 sts). Turn.
Rep row 2 until a total of 12 rows have been worked. Turn with 1 ch and finish block 16 with a row of 1 sl st in every st through both loops.

Block 17
Ch 1, turn piece and work dc along charcoal grey, pink, navy blue and light grey blocks.
Row 1: Work a total of 144 dc (BLO in navy sts). Turn.
Row 2: ch 1, dc 1 (BLO) in each st of row (144 sts). Turn.
Rep row 2 until a total of 12 rows have been worked. Turn with 1 ch and finish block 17 with a row of 1 sl st in every st through both loops.

Block 18
Ch 1, turn piece and work dc along charcoal grey, light grey, petrol blue and charcoal grey blocks.

Row 1: work a total of 226 dc (BLO in light grey sts). Turn.
Row 2: ch 1, dc (BLO) in every st of row (226 sts). Turn.
Rep row 2 until a total of 12 rows have been worked. Turn with 1 ch and finish block 18 with a row of 1 sl st in every st through both loops.
Break yarn and fasten off.

FINISHING
Weave in all ends.
Gently steam and press the blanket under a dry cloth without squashing the rib pattern completely flat.

Sandra's baby blanket

The baby blanket is worked in one piece and looks the same on both sides so is reversible. The design looks as if you need to work with several colours at once, but that is a deception: you work one row with one colour, then switch to another colour and so on. I used three different colours for this blanket, but you could try using all your leftover yarns that match the necessary yarn weight.

Measurements
65 x 102cm

Yarn
Sandnes Tynn Merinoull Wool, 100% merino, 175metres/50g
Colour A: curry 2537
Colour B: dark terracotta 4035
Colour C: black 1099
Quantity: 150g colour A, 150g colour B and 250g colour C

Crochet hook
3.5mm

Tension
30 sts x 30 rows = 10 x 10cm in pattern

Note
Turning chains are not counted in the total number of stitches.

The edge is a little flatter, partly because half treble crochet is slightly wider than double crochet, and partly because the pattern makes the blanket contract a little.

Change colour after each row of pattern and before turning. Pull the new colour of yarn through the loop on the hook. Then the piece can be turned and the next row in the pattern begun. Work a total of 2 ch with the new colour yarn (one ch is the colour change and the other ch is the turning stitch).

The pattern is woked in colours A, B and C.

Colour pattern: divisible by 2 + 1 sts

Row 1: colour C. 1 dc in 2nd ch from hook, *1 ch, skip 1 st, 1 dc in next st*, rep from * to * to end. Finish with 1 dc in last st.

Row 2: Change colour. 1 dc in 1st st, *1 dc in ch-space, ch 1, skip 1 st*, rep from * to * to end. Finish with 1 dc in ch-space and 1 dc in last ch.

Row 3: Change colour. 1 dc in 1st st, *1 ch, skip 1 st, 1 dc in ch-space*, rep from * to *. Finish with 1 ch, skip 1 dc, 1 dc in last st.

Rep rows 2 and 3.
Change between 3 colours.
NB: this is a lovely easy pattern. You don't have to think too much about colour changes as there is only one colour of yarn to choose after each row.

BLANKET

Work 175 ch with colour C. Begin the pattern by following the 1st row of pattern (left). Change colours from colour C to colour B, then from colour B to colour A, and finally from colour A to colour C. Rep pattern in this colour order until piece measures approx. 95cm. Finish blanket with colour C and continue to edge without breaking yarn.

EDGE

Work edge with colour C and make 6 rounds with htr as explained below. There are rounded corners on the worked edge. The blanket is the same on both sides, so there is no RS and WS.

Round 1: 1 htr in every st and every ch-space at beg and end of blanket. Crochet 1 htr in each row end along sides. In each of the four corner stitches on blanket work 3 htr. Close round with 1 sl st in 1st htr through both loops. Turn and work the opposite way around – now and on the next 5 rounds.

From round 2 work BLO.

Round 2: 2 ch, 1 htr BLO in every st, except 1 inc in each of the 3 sts in the four corners. Turn.
Round 3: ch 2, 1 htr BLO in every st, but 1 inc in every 2nd of the 6 sts in the four corners. Turn.
Round 4: ch 2, 1 htr BLO in every st but 1 inc in every 3rd of the 9 sts in the four corners. Turn.
Round 5: Ch 2, 1 htr BLO in every st but 1 inc in every 4th of the 12 sts in the four corners. Turn.
Round 6: Ch 2, 1 htr BLO in every st but 1 inc in every 5th of the 15 sts in the four corners. Turn.

Finish piece with a round where you work 1 ch (turn stitch), 1 sl st in every st. Break yarn and fasten off.

FINISHING

Weave in all ends.
Gently steam and press the blanket under a dry cloth.

Philip's baskets

These crochet baskets are useful for the changing table and to keep baby's things together: pacifiers, wipes, nappies and other small items. There are four sizes to make. Each one is worked with double yarn, which stiffens the basket. The yarn type is Rowan's mercerised cotton, which is more durable than regular cotton and creates a very distinct and beautiful stitch pattern. The crocheted bobbles can be omitted if you prefer a minimalist look.

Yarn
Rowan Cotton Glacé, 100% mercerised cotton, 115 metres/50g
Colour: grey 831, matt yellow 730
Quantity: 200 (250) 300 (300)g

Crochet hook
4mm

Tension
19 htr BLO x 14 rounds =10 x 10cm

Note
Bottom of basket is worked with double crochet.
Work BLO from round 2 on sides of basket unless otherwise stated in pattern. To achieve the ribbed effect on the basket, work half treble crochets alternately on every other round from RS/outside and from WS/inside of basket.

Pattern with bobbles
Work 4 incomplete tr in one st (omit last pull-through in each tr) – there are then 5 loops on hook. Wrap yarn around hook and pull through 5 loops at once.
NB: the loops should be relatively loose and of equal length on the thick part of the hook – pull the loops down and straighten them with your left hand. This will help the yarn slip through the 5 loops more easily. This also makes for a nice big bobble. Tighten so the bobble gathers and protrudes at back of piece (i.e. on RS of basket), 1 dc in next 3 sts (dc should also be tightened as it forces bobble to arch). Rep alternately 1 bobble stitch + 3 dc.

The right-hand basket is 20cm high (bottom is 20cm in diameter). The left-hand basket is 18cm high (bottom is 18cm in diameter).

Tip

Work a small bag following the pattern for the basket but then working a row of holes and pulling an anorak cord or a tie through the 4th last row.

BOTTOM

Round 1 (RS): start with two strands of yarn and a magic circle with 6 dc. Close round with 1 sl st in 1st dc. Insert a sl st at the beginning of round.
Then work dc in the round in spiral from RS through both loops with 6 incs on every round.

Do not work one increase on top of the other from round to round. Work evenly so that the bottom is rounded and smooth rather than jagged.
When working in the round in spiral, do not close round with a sl st; continue working without visible transition and without a turning ch. Just keep track of the stitch marker so you know exactly where one round ends and a new round begins.

Round 2: 1 inc in every st (12 sts).
Round 3: 1 inc in every 2nd st (18 sts).
Round 4: 1 inc in every 3rd st (24 sts).

Rep round 4, increasing the number of dc by 1 st between each of the 6 incs from one round to the next.
Work inc in every 4th, 5th, 6th, 7th st, etc.

When bottom measures 14 (16) 18 (20)cm in diameter (number of stitches is divisible by 6 sts regardless of size), work 1 round with 1 sl st in every st.

The slip stitch forms an edge that marks the transition between the bottom and sides of the basket.
Do not break the yarn.

SIDES OF THE BASKET

Round 1 (RS): 1 sl st in stitch space behind sl st edge, ch 2, 1 htr in same st, 1 htr in every st in the round (number of stitches varies and depends on size of bottom of basket). Close round with 1 sl st in 1st htr. Turn and work the opposite way around.

Round 2 (WS): 2 ch, 1 htr in every st (remember to work BLO from now on), close round with 1 sl st in 1st htr through both loops. Turn.

Rep round 2 alternately from RS and WS until piece measures 4 (5) 5 (5)cm in height from bottom.

On next round from WS work 1 ch, 1 dc, work pattern with bobbles through both loops (see page 218).
After round with bobbles work a round with 1 dc in every st from RS – again through both loops.

Now rep round 2 alternately from RS and WS on rest of piece until desired height of basket. Work a height so that there is enough for a fold.
Finish the edge from RS with 1 sl st in every st through both loops.
For a hanging loop along the edge of sl sts, work 20 ch and then work into it with 1 sl st in every ch. The strap is useful if you want to hang the basket from a hook.

FINISHING

Weave in all ends.
Gently steam and press the basket under a dry cloth.

The white bag is crocheted in double crochet using 6 skeins of 50g. Anorak cord secures the top. Measurements: 20cm in diameter and 25cm high.

Tip

Use a 3.5mm crochet hook and a single strand of Rowan Cotton Glacé for a lighter look on the small bag.

Jack's cloth and nursing pads

You can never have too many cloths. This cloth is crocheted in mercerised cotton, a type of cotton yarn given a special treatment to make it more durable. The yarn looks more shiny than ordinary cotton yarn. This design matches the crocheted baskets, p. 218, and includes a round of bobbles for decoration.

Measurements
Diameter: 22cm

Yarn
Rowan Cotton Glacé, 100% mercerised cotton, 115 metres/50g
Colour: 726 white
Quantity: approx. 50g

Crochet hook
3.5mm

Tension
25 dc BLO x 26 rounds = 10 x 10cm

Note
Make sure increases are spaced from round to round. Do not place the increases on top of each other, as this will make the cloth hexagonal rather than circular.
Turning chains do not count towards the total number of stitches.

Pattern
Work dc BLO, starting from round 2, unless otherwise stated in pattern.

Pattern with bobbles
Work 4 incomplete tr in one st (omit last pull through in each tr) – there are then 5 loops on hook. Wrap yarn around hook and pull through 5 loops at once.
NB: loops should be relatively loose and of equal length on the thick part of the hook – pull the loops down and straighten them with your left hand. This will help the yarn slip through the 5 loops more easily. It also makes a nice big bobble. Tighten so the bobble gathers and protrudes on the back of the piece (i.e. on RS of cloth), 1 dc in the next 3 sts (dc should also be tightened as it forces the bobble to arch). Rep alternately 1 bobble stitch + 3 dc.

*Nursing pads in two
different sizes.*

Tip

Good alternative yarns are Krea Deluxe Organic Cotton or Gepard Linen Unika. Cotton, linen and bamboo yarn scraps, or a yarn type with a blend of these fibres, would also be suitable.

CLOTH

Round 1 (RS): make a magic ring with 6 dc. Close with 1 sl st in 1st dc.
Turn, then work the opposite way around – now and on all rounds on cloth.
Round 2 (WS): ch 1, dc (remember to work BLO from now on), inc 1 in every st around. Close round with 1 sl st in 1st dc through both loops (12 sts).
Round 3 (RS): ch 1, *1 dc, inc 1*, rep from * to * around, and close round with 1 sl st in 1st dc, as described before, now and on all rounds on cloth (18 sts).
Round 4 (WS): ch 1, *2 dc, inc 1*, rep from * to * around (24 sts).

Rep rounds 3 and 4 with incs, increasing by 1 st between incs from round to round. So, for example, round 5 will be: ch 1, * 3 dc, inc 1*, rep from * to * around (32 sts); round 6 will be: ch 1, * 4dc, inc 1 * rep from * to * around (38 sts).
Work 6 incs on every round from 2nd round – work until there are 23 rounds in total on cloth (138 sts in total).

Round 24 (WS): ch 1, work pattern with bobbles through both loops (see p. 222).
Round 25 (RS): ch 1, dc in every st through both loops and 12 incs evenly spaced (inc was omitted on round 24, so these 6 incs need to be made up) (150 sts).

Rounds 26–30: ch 1, dc in every st BLO and 6 incs evenly spaced.

There are 180 sts in total after round 30.

Round 31 (RS): ch 1, 1 sl st in every st through both loops. If desired, work a hanging loop of 25 ch and work into it with sl sts at the same time as working a final round of sl st.
Break yarn and fasten off.

FINISHING
Weave in all ends.
Gently smooth and steam the cloth under a dry cloth. Do not flatten bobbles and dc rib.

NURSING PADS
Refer to the tip opposite to work the nursing pads. Use a suitable yarn and follow the instructions for Jack's cloth until each pad is 11–12cm or desired size.

Tip

I worked as a nurse in a maternity ward in the late 1990s, and lanolin nursing pads were then, as now, very useful for new mothers. Crochet a nursing insert as a small cloth 11–12cm in diameter (without bobbles) in lanolin yarn from Askeladen. You can, of course, crochet them in any other size you wish. You will then have the best, warmest and softest nursing pads in the world. Make two of them – more if you like. Use a hook that matches the thickness of your lanolin yarn. Lanolin has anti-inflammatory and antibacterial properties. It lubricates the skin and helps to make it soft and resistant. These pads also keep the breasts warm between feedings to prevent breast inflammation. The inserts don't need frequent washing. In fact, they don't really need washing at all; just a gentle rinse once in a while without soap. You might think that's not true, but the liners don't smell, even after getting wet with breast milk repeatedly. You can complement the wound-healing properties of lanolin with a lanolin cream if there are scratches and sores on the breasts.

Bjørn's coat-hanger cover

A special hanger for baby clothes. This is a quick and easy crochet project that lends itself well to leftover yarn. Here I used a durable and affordable yarn.

Yarn
Drops Cotton Light, 50% cotton and 50% polyester, 105 metres/50g
Colour: dark grey, unicolour 30
Quantity: approx. 20g

Other materials
Small hanger

Crochet hook
3.5mm

Note
Work the equivalent of a small tube into which the hanger can be inserted (as with Holger's pacifier cord, p. 204). The assembly on the round must be placed under the hanger so that it cannot be seen.

Cover
Measure the length and circumference of the hanger; work the number of chain stitches that corresponds to the circumference of the hanger (the cover should be firm and not too loose).

Make the given number of ch to form a ring closed with 1 sl st.

Round 1: ch 1 (turning chain) and then dc 1 in every ch in the round.

Close round with 1 sl st in 1st dc.

Round 2: ch 1, and now work the other way round with dc BLO. Close round with 1 sl st in the 1st dc through both loops. Turn.

Rep round 2 with dc BLO until cover measures halfway up hanger.

If the hook on the hanger can be unscrewed, work a small hole on cover by working 1 or 2 ch and skipping 1 or 2 sts so that the hook can be screwed back in place when the cover is put on. If the hook cannot be removed, work two identical pieces of cover and work them together under the hook in the middle with sl sts from RS.

Place the cover on the hanger.

If you are working with the Drops Cotton Light yarn, use a 3.5mm hook.

FINISHING
Close the cover at both ends by working sts together 2 by 2 with dc through both layers and finally edge with 1 sl st in each dc through both loops. Weave in the ends.

Acknowledgements

First of all, many thanks to Marie Brocks Larsen at Turbine Publishers, for believing in my book.

A special thanks to the editor, Camilla Lyng, for guiding me through the process to produce a better and more readable book. The editing was a tough slog with a million details to deal with along the way.

Many thanks to Sandnes, Gepard (Uldstedet), Permin, Lang Yarn, Cewec, Krea Deluxe and Önling for their trust, support and supplying the beautiful yarns for the book.

Many thanks to family, friends and especially my students for their help and encouraging comments along the way.

Many thanks to Louise Gram, needlework editor at Hendes Verden, for help, advice and encouragement when I have been in doubt along the way. It was Louise who got me started writing crochet patterns.

Many hugs and thanks to my sister, Karina Kofoed Bæk, and my FOF colleague, Susanne Kronholm Mathiasen, for their help, invaluable crochet time and great ideas.

Sandra Javadi @sandrajavadi and Mette Ørskov @idocrea have been faithful and enthusiastic test crocheters – thank you so much for great feedback. Sandra has also provided the gorgeous babies for the photo shoot.

About the author

Charlotte Kofoed Westh learned to crochet and knit from her grandmother during long holidays on Bornholm in the 1970s. Her grandmother, Agnes Marie Westh, was an honorary member of the Sewing Association and could crochet and embroider the most beautiful things. It was all neat and finely made, and she took great care with the details. Charlotte has inherited this attention to detail as evident in the beautiful edges, the good drape and the comfortable fit that all her designs have in common.

As a child, Charlotte spent many hours in the company of her grandmother and mother's yarn scraps, experimenting with crocheting and knitting clothes for dolls and making gifts for her family. But as she couldn't read a pattern in the early years, she was left to her own imagination and creativity. It wasn't until high school that she learned to decipher patterns from magazines and became truly obsessed with knitting and crocheting – even to the point of always bringing yarn to class.

Forty years later, Charlotte is still obsessed with yarn, and handwork has gone from hobby to full-time job. Today, Charlotte teaches knitting and crochet at FOF Køge Bugt and designs for Egmont Publishing, which publishes her crochet and knitting patterns in Hjemmet, Hendes Verden and Sally's.

First published in the United Kingdom in 2023 by
B.T. Batsford Ltd
43 Great Ormond Street
London WC1N 3HZ
An imprint of B.T. Batsford Holdings Ltd

ISBN: 978 1 84994 806 7

A CIP catalogue record for this book is available from the
British Library.

33 32 31 30 29 28 27 26 25 24 23
10 9 8 7 6 5 4 3 2 1

Reproduction by Rival Colour Ltd, UK
Printed and bound by Leo Paper Products, China

This book can be ordered direct from the publisher at
www.batsfordbooks.com